SO WHY ARE YOU STILL PADDLING?

Learning how to Trust

Hiba.
No matter what....''
Trust God and all
that he has for you.
Blessings of abundance.
Over flowing.
full of grace.

Barbara Mikus

All my love 'sister'
Barbara Mikus

SO WHY ARE YOU STILL PADDLING?

Printed in Canada

ISBN: 978-1-4866-0005-2

Word Alive Press
131 Cordite Road, Winnipeg, MB R3W 1S1
www.wordalivepress.ca

MIX
Paper from
responsible sources
FSC
www.fsc.org   FSC® C016245

Cataloguing in Publication information may be obtained through Library and Archives Canada.

TABLE
OF
CONTENTS

ACKNOWLEDGEMENTS

I thank God for the many trials and difficult circumstances He has placed in my life, because I know each of them has tested my faith. Through this testing, increasing measures of perseverance have been produced in my life. When I allow perseverance to finish its work, I find that I've become a more mature believer who doesn't lack anything. If God hadn't allowed these challenges to occur in my life, I wouldn't have needed to learn to trust Him.

Little did I know that, during a time of frustration at my husband's lack of zeal for spiritual matters, God would use my flippant remarks as permission to bring new trials into my life. Be careful what you pray for. I said, "God, you created my husband. Therefore, Jim is Your problem, not mine. I cannot change him. Only You can." It wasn't until well into my journey of trusting God that I realized I had, in fact, given God permission to bring these challenges.

I thank Holy Spirit for being my comforter and coming alongside me as I faced the many trials of my Christian walk. Whoever said that Christianity is a crutch doesn't fully understand that being a Christian is difficult. Choosing to embrace the teachings found in the scriptures and being a true disciple of Jesus Christ is much more difficult than choosing to live a life without God. Choosing to trust is much more difficult than choosing to control. Yet the rewards are far greater.

To my husband, I thank you for allowing God to continue to perfect His work in you. Since we have reconciled, I have watched you grow and mature in the ways of God. I have witnessed your road to Damascus experience (in our case, Mesquite), when God's calling on your life became clear and articulate. I wait patiently to see how God will unfold His good and perfect will for your life. We have recently celebrated twenty years of marriage. I look forward to seeing how God works in our relationship during the next twenty years.

To my family and friends, I thank you for your prayers, encouragement, and support. As I've walked through the many trials God has allowed me to face, you have ensured that I was never alone. You prayed for me when I never even knew you were thinking about me. You have helped me to continue walking forward when everything in me wanted to retreat. Your arms embraced me when I cried and your shoulders were available for me to lean on when I could stand no longer.

To Josie and Carolyn, thank you for being there! Thank you for the intercessory prayers you offered during the six months of my separation. You had a significant part in the writing of this book. Without you in my life and by my side, I may not have known the victory, and I certainly wouldn't have had a testimony about trusting God to share with other believers.

To Kenn and Cheryl and the leadership team of the Ripple Centre, thank you for keeping me accountable and ensuring that I didn't retreat. Thank you for helping me persevere one day at a time, one step at a time.

To my work colleagues, thank you for your patience and under-standing as you watched God perform a miracle in my marriage.

Finally, to my anonymous encouragers, thank you for your continual curiosity and prompting on when I was going to write another book.

FOREWORD

It is with great honor that we write this second forward for Barb's second book. Our journey with Barb is just shy of 30 years.

Barb has been and continues to be a good friend, a woman of God, a devout follower of Jesus Christ and very passionate about her personal relationship with Him. She also possesses a strong desire to assist other Jesus Followers in their journey of faith.

As a spiritual daughter, she continues to cause our heart to be moistened by her honest, upfront, committed relationship with Jesus. As I read this manuscript several times throughout numerous edits I found myself weeping tears of joy. The unfolding story of her Trust in God while she continues to '*Paddle Her Own Canoe*' is heart warming, challenging and fully authentic.

We have watched her 'paddle'. We were eyewitnesses to the outworking of a modern day relational miracle that is profiled in this second book. I heard a man of God state many years ago that there is 'no such thing as a day of miracles, just a God of miracle-working POWER.' This book embodies that message.

Barb has endeavored to write this book in such a way that it can be used personally or in a group setting as a bible study. She discovers and examines a series of bible characters who were also 'paddling their canoes'. These characters come alive as she identifies with them in their journeys of faith and invites us to learn from them and follow their example.

This book is also a testimony to the power of light over the power of darkness. Barb is still paddling because her faith in Christ remained strong in the midst of heart wrenching trials. The good news is: as she Trusted God, He worked a miracle of reconciliation which in the modern era is very powerful. Enjoy the canoe ride.

Kenn & Cheryl Gill
The Ripple Centre, Network Family & Stream
Calgary, Alberta

INTRODUCTION

Salvation gets you into the canoe.
Relationship helps you stay in the canoe.
Trust shows you *when* to paddle your canoe.

Some trust in chariots and some in horses, but we trust in the name of the Lord our God. (Psalm 20:7)
Yet you brought me out of the womb; you made me trust in you, even at my mother's breast. (Psalm 22:9)

In my first book, *Who's Paddling Your Canoe?*, I compared our Christian journey to a canoe expedition. During the voyage, we are passengers while Jesus is the guide. The first step, leaving the shore, illustrates salvation. Learning to paddle in the rapids illustrates perseverance. Various stops along the way illustrate discipleship, forgiveness, and trust.

The successful surrender of the paddles indicates who's in control as Christian attributes such as patience, honour, love, joy, and hope develop in our lives. Add the need for relationships and the desire to be involved in ministry and the reader learns that the journey can be exciting and rewarding. Different events along the voyage represent specific stages in our lives when we need to make choices. The results are based upon who's paddling the canoe. The journey can take as long as required, or may not be completed at all.

This first book has become a great introductory Bible study for many new believers, as well as a source of encouragement for many who are looking for strength along their own journeys. In addition, I've learned that this book has become a great witnessing tool for those seeking the kingdom of God.

Over the past few years, as my relationship with Jesus Christ has matured, I have realized that each of the chapters in the first book could, in fact, become a book of its own. When we study the scriptures about each of these attributes, we realize that the levels of revelation get deeper and deeper.

One attribute in particular, and one that has become the recurring theme of the first book, is trust. Devoting less than ten pages on the subject was truly only an introduction, a commentary that barely scratched the surface. One of my favourite scriptures has become Proverbs 3:5—*"Trust in the Lord with all your heart and lean not on your own understanding."* This is an easy scripture to quote, but what exactly does it mean? What does trust look like? With all my heart… does that mean without my head? Simply speaking, yes. As the verse says, we are not to lean on our own understanding. In other words, we don't lean on our own knowledge, wisdom, or circumstances. Trust is different than hope and belief, even though these words are often interchangeable.

Hope. To me, this word sounds like a wish. In other words, I expect, anticipate, and look forward to a successful outcome.

Believe. To me, this word sounds more like a proclamation—a certainty. In other words, I accept something as true. I have faith and do not doubt. I believe (I do not doubt) that God will never leave me or forsake me.

Trust. To me, this word represents a conviction, a reliance, or a dependence. Even though a thesaurus indicates that "hope" and "faith" can be used in the place of "trust," I disagree. Hope and faith sound like something I can *have* (i.e. a noun), whereas trust sounds like something I *do* (i.e. a verb). In other words, trust has a posture. I choose to trust, no matter the circumstances or outcome, because I know that all things work together for the good of those who are called for His purposes. The wish (hope) may not be granted. The statement (believe) may not be fulfilled, but my trust will endure forever.

This book deals with the matter of trust. What do you trust? Why do you trust? Who should you trust? Where and when do you trust? Most importantly, how do you trust? What is your posture?

Years may have passed since that memorable decision. You may have had many seasons of paddling and many seasons of being still. Some of these seasons may have been God-ordained. Others may have seen you paddle out of rebellion or ignorance.

This book will provide ten biblical examples of how people trusted God. Each of their situations was different. How they chose to trust God was also different. My reason for choosing these specific individuals is to show you that when you're in a position of leadership or influence, you can still choose to trust God. To illustrate this point, I compare each of their situations with a workplace setting in my own life. In most of these situations, I was working in a secular organization where everything around me said I needed to be in control. However, when we choose to trust and give up control, God's outcome turns out to be much better than anything we could have come up with.

The second most difficult area to trust to God is our relationships, especially our marriages. Through the study of each of these biblical examples, I illustrate how I learned to trust God in my marriage. When God asks, "So why are you still paddling?" remember that He is in control. We must put down our paddles and let God lead in these two significant areas our lives—not just sometimes, but all the time.

I'm getting ahead of myself. God allowed a very significant event in my life so I could learn how to trust Him—I mean, *really* trust him. However, before we get too far into my story, I'd like to establish a foundation of how we usually trust and what we trust in.

WHAT ARE YOU TRUSTING?

For many of us, trust goes with something we know, see, and understand. Trust is proven. Trust is synonymous with the statement that says that for every action, there is an equal reaction. When I throw a ball, I trust (I know) that the other player will catch the ball. When I see a tractor on an ice-covered lake, I trust (I know) that the ice is safe enough for me skate on. When I study for an exam, I trust (I know) that I'll be rewarded with a good grade. When I start to diet and exercise more regularly, I trust (I know) that I'll lose weight and be in better physical shape. When I turn off the bedroom lamp, I trust (I know) that the room will be dark enough for me to sleep. When I plant my vegetable garden, I trust (I know) that the corn seeds I planted will grow into stalks of corn and not vines of tomatoes. When I travel on an airplane, I trust (I know) that the pilot is able to fly the plane safely.

Are you starting to understand what I'm saying? Trust is easy when it's based on what we know, see, and understand in the physical sense. However, God is a spirit, not a physical being. We cannot see God's lips move when He speaks to us. We cannot feel God holding our hand, yet we know He's always with us. His word says that He will never leave us or forsake us. How do you learn to trust what you cannot see? How do you learn to trust what you cannot understand? Truly trusting God may mean ignoring logic and responding to situations in a manner that appears foolish to those around you, especially the nonbelievers in your midst.

If you're like me, you've spent many years "in the world" where you didn't trust God. You may have been angry at Him, or you may have even believed that He didn't care or possibly didn't even exist at all. As a result, you learned to trust in something else. More likely than not, you learned to trust in yourself.

Scriptures for Reflection

There are several illustrations in God's word of where we can place our trust. As you read each of these scriptures, reflect upon your own life and discover where you may have placed your trust in the past.

1. Idols (Possessions)
I hate those who cling to worthless idols; I trust in the Lord. (Psalm 31:6)

But those who trust in idols, who say to images, "You are our gods," will be turned back in utter shame. (Isaiah 42:17)

Of what value is an idol, since a man has carved it? Or an image that teaches lies? For he who makes it trusts in his own creation; he makes idols that cannot speak. (Habakkuk 2:18)

----

2. Friends and Family
   Even my close friend, whom I trusted, he who shared my bread, has lifted up his heel against me. (Psalm 41:9)

   It is better to take refuge in the Lord than to trust in man. (Psalm 118:8)

   Beware of your friends; do not trust your brothers. For every brother is a deceiver, and every friend a slanderer. (Jeremiah 9:4)

   _____

   _____

   _____

   _____

   _____

   _____

3. Weapons
   What he trusts in is fragile; what he relies on is a spider's web. (Job 8:14)

   I do not trust in my bow, my sword does not bring me victory. (Psalm 44:6)

   Why do you boast of your valleys, boast of your valleys so fruitful? O unfaithful daughter, you trust in your riches and say, "Who will attack me?" (Jeremiah 49:4)

   _____

   _____

   _____

   _____

   _____

3

4. Wealth and Beauty

Here now is the man who did not make God his stronghold but trusted in his great wealth and grew strong by destroying others! (Psalm 52:7)

Do not trust in extortion or take pride in stolen goods; though your riches increase, do not set your heart on them. (Psalm 62:10)

Whoever trusts in his riches will fall, but the righteous will thrive like a green leaf. (Proverbs 11:28)

_____

_____

_____

_____

_____

_____

5. Yourself (Knowledge)

He who trusts in himself is a fool, but he who walks in wisdom is kept safe. (Proverbs 28:26)

You have trusted in your wickedness and have said, "No one sees me." Your wisdom and knowledge mislead you when you say to yourself, "I am, and there is none besides me." (Isaiah 47:10)

She obeys no one, she accepts no correction. She does not trust in the Lord, she does not draw near to her God. (Zephaniah 3:2)

_____

_____

_____

_____

_____

_____

6. Leadership

> *It is better to take refuge in the Lord than to trust in princes.*
> (Psalm 118:9)

> *Those who trusted in Cush and boasted in Egypt will be afraid and put to shame.* (Isaiah 20:5)

> *Woe to those who go down to Egypt for help, who rely on horses, who trust in the multitude of their chariots and in the great strength of their horsemen, but do not look to the Holy One of Israel, or seek help from the Lord.* (Isaiah 31:1)

_____

_____

_____

_____

_____

_____

MY STORY

For the first thirty years of my life, I trusted in all of the above, but most prevalently in myself. I was the eldest daughter of a farmer who was forced to marry his high school sweetheart when she got pregnant at the age of seventeen. I spent my first fifteen years living in poverty, in an old uninsulated farmhouse without running water. However, I didn't think of our family as poor because everyone else in our community was in the same situation. Then, at the age of fifteen, my parents separated and my mom moved to the nearest city, taking myself and my three younger siblings with her. Since my mom had never worked anywhere but on the farm, she had no marketable skills she could rely on to support her children. Poverty still plagued my father, so child support was sporadic and alimony nonexistent. With a part-time job as a dishwasher, Mom was able to earn enough money to pay for a low-rental house in the east end of town.

Being taken away from my friends at the start of high school proved to be a critical point in my life. An attitude of rebellion started to set in. Nobody asked me if I wanted to move. If I had been given a choice, I may have elected to stay with my dad. I realize that living with my dad would have been unhealthy, as his aberrant sexual influence would have led to an even greater impact on my life. Because I wasn't given a choice, I rebelled. I fell in with the wrong crowd, enjoying the social scene rather than applying myself to my studies.

In order to fit into this new crowd, I chose to trust in everything but God. The God of my Sunday school years certainly wasn't around. If he had been, my situation wouldn't have been the way it was. Instead I chose to trust in idols in the form of music, things I collected that were "mine," the peace symbols of the 70s, and my daily horoscope. I trusted in my friends. We drank together before school dances and skipped classes when we thought we could get away with it. I became the captain of the cheerleading squad so I could be popular, especially with the boys on the basketball team. I wanted to fit in. I wanted my social position to bring me to a place of trust.

Although we were living on the wrong side of the tracks, I didn't want my peers to think of me as poor. Since I didn't have any money, I stole so I could have the right clothes and make-up. I wanted to appear wealthy. Thankfully, due to a friend telling her father—or maybe it was my mother confiding in a neighbour—I was given "the speech" during a ride to school one day. I quickly changed my ways, not wanting to be turned in to the local authorities. I obtained a part-time job. If I wanted nice clothes and the money to be able to do things with my new friends, I needed to earn it for myself. Money certainly wasn't going to come from either of my parents.

Yes, I also trusted in my beauty and sexual prowess. I was able to date any boy I wanted and broke up with many of them on a whim. Why? Because I was the one in control. Nobody was going to dump me; I always dumped them first. Nobody was going to seduce me; I would seduce them first.

Finally, I trusted in my leadership ability. From a very young age, I was taught to be independent and to lead others. I was babysitting before I was nine years old. I was responsible for family meals from the age of ten. I was the president of our 4-H Club when I was only fourteen. I was in a position of influence at summer camps and I was given supervisory duties in my first full-time job before I'd even had my first annual performance review.

Me, myself, and I didn't need to trust in God. I could do it my way and be proud of it. When I was passed up for a Junior Accounting job at the age of nineteen, I vowed that I would show them. I wasn't going to be like my mom, penniless with four children at the age of thirty-three. I was going to get a degree in business and become a chartered accountant. I was going to become a person of influence, able to exercise power and authority when needed and never need to rely on anyone for my happiness. I was going to be able to use my education to get any job I wanted and lead whatever lifestyle I chose.

GROUP DISCUSSION

Share a situation where you leaned on your own understanding and didn't trust in God. What were the results?

WHEN DO YOU LEARN TO TRUST?

2

Many of us need to cry "Help me!" before we cry out for God. Our plea may be verbalized, or it may just be an expression on our face revealing the agony within our hearts. We want to be set free from severe difficulties in our lives. Seemingly innumerable problems plague us over and over again. We just cannot seem to break free.

The enemy may have us in bondage. We look for someone to listen to our stories. Our friends are no longer willing to listen, so we seek professional counsel. The meditation and medicine they prescribe don't respond to our inner cries. When we've finally done everything we know and understand to do, and realize that our actions and pursuits are in vain, we cry out to God. We willingly, albeit in desperation, begin the process of salvation and acknowledge first and foremost that we need a Saviour, that we need Jesus to intervene in the mess we've made of our lives. Being "in control" hasn't led to success. Instead it has led to devastation and destruction.

1. WHEN YOU ARE ABANDONED OR REJECTED

The institutions of home and marriage are being severely attacked today. Satan is working in many lives and marriage problems continue to become more numerous.

We have a strong tendency toward selfishness. Individuals think in terms of receiving rather than giving. Along with selfishness, they lean toward blaming others for and excusing themselves of faults and mistakes. Such indulgence in self-pity only short-circuits their faith in God. As judgment increases, love decreases. God can work out our problems in marvellous and redemptive ways even when there seems to be no hope.

Sometimes demonic forces cause an individual to become involved in alcohol, unfaithfulness, lack of consideration, and even cruelty in a relationship. Some individuals are undoubtedly the victims of gross sins on the part of others. Often there are two sides to the matter, but there are times when demonic forces oppress us in unusual ways.

The best way to be healed from abandonment and rejection is to *forgive*. Is Jesus prompting you to be healed from the anger and bitterness caused by abandonment or rejection? Is Jesus asking you to forgive? Yes, He is. However, you remember that you vowed not to see or speak to the person who wronged you. Who is this person? Did he hurt you? Abandon you? Abuse you—physically, sexually, or emotionally? Did he steal from you—a relationship, possessions, or take credit for your deeds? Is he more successful than you? Are you jealous or envious of him? Is he involved in a lifestyle you struggle with wanting to be part of again? Does this person represent that secret room of your heart Jesus isn't allowed to enter?

Perhaps you cannot forgive that person for what he did. However, by trusting Holy Spirit, you'll be led through the process of forgiveness and be fully released from your feelings of abandonment and rejection.

Through the patience and love of Jesus, He begins to show you that you must be healed to be set free. You must forgive others to experience the forgiveness that comes from the Father. Jesus already knows those secret places of your heart. He already knows what tempts you. He wants to set you free. What is this secret place? Who can you not forgive? What is that hidden sin?

- A father, uncle, or brother who sexually abused you and stole your innocence?
- A boyfriend or husband who physically abused you?

- A sibling who always got what she wanted, who always did everything right, the star, the successful one, the favourite?
- A boss or co-worker who picked on you, bullied you, took glory for your work and ideas?
- A friend who hurt you many years ago by leaving you out, taking your boyfriend or husband?

Or is this a secret sin?
- Promiscuity or pornography?
- Obsessive compulsive behaviour?
- Depression and anxiety?
- Greed and lust?

By trusting in the Lord's help, you can overcome. This will be a painful experience, but with the lover of your soul beside you, the ending will be better than the beginning. Trust begins to build its foundation.

2. WHEN YOU HAVE BACKSLIDDEN

When we are convicted of failing the Lord and backsliding, we may easily have a sense of severe guilt and condemnation. The Spirit of God moves to convict us of sin, but Satan comes to bring oppressing condemnation. Sometimes we may feel like there is no hope. God, in His love and mercy, wants to forgive us. As the people were told in Hosea 14:4, the Lord would heal their waywardness.

As we repent of our sins, God forgives. When God forgives, He forgets and put those sins under the blood of Jesus. We must accept this forgiveness and also forgive ourselves. The joy and blessings of fellowship with the Lord we have been hindered from experiencing can be restored.

We must remember that for our true Christian journey to begin, we must leave our former life. We must accept that God loves us. He has a plan for us. He wants to bless us.

Therefore, no matter what has happened, no matter what the Lord has taken you away from, or has taken away from you, this is God's will for this time in your life. God has called you back to Him, and only Him. What caused you to backslide?

- A failed marriage?
- An inappropriate relationship?
- A lost friendship?
- The death of a parent or spouse?
- The loss of a child?
- The comfort of the lifestyle you used to lead? (In North America, this may be routed in materialism, the lifestyle of wanting to collect more things.)
- An inappropriate work setting?
- An illegal, dishonest, deceitful, or immoral business arrangement?

Jesus wants us to get away from all the things that distract us. He wants to have a relationship with us.

3. WHEN YOU ARE IN CRITICAL CIRCUMSTANCES

We aren't immune to difficulties. Trusting the Lord doesn't mean we'll be completely isolated from problems. There are many afflictions of the righteous, but the Lord delivers us out of them all. Going through difficulties results in a refining process, because God can work redemption in all circumstances. Regardless of the circumstances that develop, or the reasons for them, God can work in our particular situations for our own good if we truly love and trust Him.

God will help us with our burdens today. We are not to think about tomorrow's problems and borrow those difficulties. Don't concentrate on the problem. Look up and away from it. God is bigger than our problems. He can easily help us solve them, just as He stilled the storm for the disciples. A solution will become clear as we pray and believe God and exercise faith.

Sometimes our conditions cannot change, but our attitudes can. This, in turn, may change our circumstances. God knows of our difficulties and problems, and He has answers. If we trust Him, He will direct our paths.

Are you being asked to persevere during a time that you're confident you've been prepared and trained for? Perhaps you thought you'd experienced the worst that life has to offer but now realize that the most difficult challenges seem to be ahead of you. Or maybe you realize that you're in the middle of your nightmare already.

- Maybe you've lost your job.
- Maybe one of your parents has recently been diagnosed with Alzheimer's and your siblings have agreed that you're the most likely candidate for fulfilling the caregiving role.
- Maybe your teenage daughter tells you she's pregnant.
- Maybe you discover that your adolescent son has been caught selling drugs.
- Maybe your husband confesses to an affair.
- Maybe you've been diagnosed with cancer.

As James 1:2 states, we are to consider it pure joy whenever we face trials of many kinds (difficult circumstances), because this testing of our faith produces perseverance. We must let perseverance finish its work so that we may be mature and complete, not lacking anything.

In addition, Romans 5:3 states that we are to glory in our sufferings (critical circumstances), because we know that this suffering will produce perseverance. Perseverance will then develop our character. Our character will lead to hope, and hope will not produce shame. In other words, when we face critical situations and difficulties, the result *will not* be shame. The result will be the development of our character to continually focus on Jesus Christ, our hope of glory.

4. WHEN YOU ARE DEALING WITH DEATH OR EXPERIENCING DEPRESSION

One of the many causes of severe grief is the death of a loved one. This is a time of loneliness. In times like these, we must not question God but place our utmost confidence in Him. Tragedy must not be blamed on God; rather, Satan comes to kill, steal, destroy, and take away. Regardless of how bad the circumstances are, God can redeem the situation. His grace is sufficient for us.

We may walk through a very deep valley, but we cannot look back. We must press forward and move ahead. We can come to new mountaintop experiences of God's blessings and experience His glory in new ways. We must trust the Lord completely and commit our futures to Him. He will soothe the heart that is mourning and give comfort. We must learn to continually believe God in the midst of any discouragement. The peace of His Spirit will overcome the loneliness that engulfs us. God will give us strength and peace.

There may be other times when the dark depths of depression seem to draw us away and hide from the world around us. Perhaps there is no joy in your life and you can no longer even pretend to care about what's happening around you. You don't want to play anymore. You want to fall asleep and hope that you don't wake up. The darker the blanket, the better!

Depression usually occurs when we're facing trials. Instead of counting these trials as pure joy, we perceive them as a form of penance. We think we've done something wrong and that God is punishing us. Much like our earthly fathers may have done, we are being disciplined. We begin to relate to the book of Job. Our emotional health is attacked. We've been impacted by the death of loved ones and our friends have abandoned us. Some days, we may wish we had never been born. If we disappeared or died tomorrow, would anybody miss us? We may have gone beyond mere depression to the point of considering suicide.

5. WHEN YOU ARE AFRAID

Fear has devastating results. It can virtually paralyze an individual and make him helpless. It stops the flow of God's power. Fear comes down to believing the wrong thing. Dependence on God, a right relationship with Him, and the daily practice of faith will overcome fear.

Sometimes a spirit of fear can oppress an individual. Fear *is* a spirit. It's a spiritual power and force we need to bind and command away in the name of Jesus. We can take authority over spiritual forces and be delivered and set free from the oppressive powers of the enemy. Believe and trust in the Lord.

Perfect love casts out all fear. At least, that's what the scriptures tell us. However, have there ever been times in our lives when love wasn't on our minds? When we were so overcome with fear that we couldn't think of anything else but mere survival?

Let me paint another picture. You have enjoyed a very calm life for quite some time. You have had no hardships. Your routine doesn't show any sign of anxiety or stress. If anything, everything seems too normal, too quiet. You can just sense that this must be the calm before the storm.

What happens when those storms of life break out? What happens when your life begins to be tossed to and fro? Do you hunker down inside your home, hiding amidst your family and holding on to your possessions? Do you feel safe and protected?

Despite doing all these things, you probably don't feel safe. You're afraid. You're afraid that the storms won't stop, that the attacks will never cease. You think, "Why do these storms always happen in the darkest of night?" You could cope with it during the daytime, because you could see what was going on, but in the night you cannot see anything. All you can do is *feel*, and it's exactly these feelings that get you into a panic, because you start to imagine the worst.

But wait a minute! You finally realize that you're not alone in this time of terror. Jesus is with you. Why is He not doing something? He should be comforting you. Holding you and telling you that everything is going to be okay. Where is He, anyway?

You slowly move away from the deceptive protection of your family and possessions. What do you discover? Yes, Jesus is still with you. But is He trying to keep your walk upright? Is He holding on to your possessions so that you won't lose them? Is He making intercessions to the Father to stop the storm so the two of you can continue your peaceful journey? No. To your absolute astonishment, Jesus seems to be asleep. He appears to not have a care in the world. This cannot be, you think! Is He unconscious? Dead? Of course not, you remember. Jesus is alive. Then what's happening? You don't understand. In your fear, you cry out to Him.

Does Jesus answer your call? Of course He does! His word says that when we call, He will answer. He will make a way where there is no way. His voice can calm the stormiest situation.

Think about your current situation. Are you succumbing to fear? Do you think Jesus isn't there? No matter the storm, He is always there.

15

There are times when He even carries you through. Do not be afraid of the dark. Do not be afraid of being alone. Do not be afraid of being poor or without food. Do not be afraid of the storms of life that come your way. It is through these storms that your faith is tried and your love for our Lord Jesus is tested and proven.

The next time you consider entering into a state of fear, call upon the name of the Lord Jesus. You'll be surprised at what happens. The storms may continue, but you'll have a peace and assurance that everything is going to be okay. Your perfect love for Him will cast out fear.

Remember, when fear comes knocking at your door, answer it with faith. When you open the door, nothing will be there.

Scriptures for Reflection

1. Abandonment and Rejection
   Wait for the Lord; be strong and take heart and wait for the Lord. (Psalm 27:14)

   He heals the broken heart and binds up their wounds. (Psalm 147:3)

   Be kind and compassionate to one another, forgiving each other, just as in Christ God forgave you. (Ephesians 4:32)

   _____

   _____

   _____

   _____

   _____

2. Backsliding
   "Come now, let us reason together," says the Lord. "Though your sins are like scarlet, they shall be as white as snow; though they are red as crimson, they shall be like wool." (Isaiah 1:18)

   And we know that in all things God works for the good of those who love him, who have been called according to his purpose. (Romans 8:28)

   The Lord will fulfill his purpose for me; your love, O Lord, endures forever—do not abandon the works of your hands. (Psalm 138:8)

   _____

   _____

   _____

   _____

17

3. Critical Circumstances

Cast your cares on the Lord and he will sustain you. (Psalm 55:22)

For I am the Lord, your God, who takes hold of your right hand... (Isaiah 41:13)

I will strengthen you and help you; I will uphold you with my righteous right hand. (Isaiah 41:10)

_____

_____

_____

_____

_____

4. Death

Be strong and courageous. Do not be terrified; do not be discouraged, for the Lord your God will be with you wherever you go. (Joshua 1:9)

As a mother comforts her child, so will I comfort you. (Isaiah 66:13)

And surely I am with you always, to the very end of the age. (Matthew 28:20)

_____

_____

_____

_____

_____

_____

_____

5. Fear

I sought the Lord, and he answered me; he delivered me from all my fears. (Psalm 34:4)

Even though I walk through the valley of the shadow of death, I will fear no evil, for you are with me. (Psalm 23:4)

For God did not give us a spirit of timidity, but a spirit of power, of love and of self-discipline. (2 Timothy 1:7)

MY STORY

Although I had been a Christian for twenty-two years and seen God do some amazing things in and through me, it took a devastating situation for me to realize that I still hadn't learned to fully trust God. There were remnants of my life where I still wanted to be in control and rely on my own understanding.

As part of promoting my book, I was asked to be a guest on *100 Huntley Street*. Since this interview would require my physical presence in Burlington, Ontario, I decided to arrange for a couple of speaking engagements and other media interviews in the area. By maximizing the potential for compensation during this time, I was able to cover my travel costs.

I was asked to be the guest preacher at a small Pentecostal church in Hamilton on the preceding Sunday. On Tuesday, I was in the *100 Huntley Street* studios. A very good friend of mine was with me to offer her silent encouragement and prayers while I was being interviewed on live television. To say that this was a grand and exciting experience would be an understatement. I could hardly believe that I, of all people, was on a television program being aired all over the world. I knew that family and friends alike were tuned in to see me and hear what I was going to share. It could easily be classified as one of the most significant highlights of my life.

That evening, I was on a flight to Winnipeg, where I was to be interviewed the following morning on *It's a New Day*. As expected, the interview was exciting. Afterwards, I headed back to the airport to continue my flight home to Calgary. With great enthusiasm, I looked forward to meeting my husband Jim at the airport.

On our way home from the airport that Wednesday afternoon, Jim indicated that he would be going for a bike ride as soon as we got home. I was rather surprised, because this was Wednesday, which meant we had our regular biweekly leadership meeting with our pastor. When I asked if Jim had forgotten this, he informed me that he had not forgotten and had no plans to attend.

His simplistic reply did little to satisfy my curiosity. Being in regular attendance at these leadership meetings was important, so why would he choose to go for a bike ride? He said we would talk about it later. Well, I wasn't willing to accept this deferral and continued to press my husband.

Then a statement came out of his mouth that I certainly did not expect: "Barb, I want a divorce."

"What are you saying?" I asked, shocked. "What has happened? Can we talk about this?"

His angry response was that we would talk about it later. He hadn't intended to bring this up, but thanks to my persistence everything was now out in the open. You can imagine what the remainder of the car ride home was like. He refused to speak to me and I was too stunned to speak to him.

Wow! What had just happened? The pinnacle of my life—the mountaintop experience I had wanted to share with him—had just been squashed. Blown away… stolen.

When I was home and Jim had left for his bike ride, I chose to make three very important phone calls. The first call was to my pastor to inform him of what Jim had just advised me and that I would likely not be at the leadership meeting that evening. Even though I had so much to share about the *100 Huntley Street* experience, and even though I knew everyone would be full of questions, my mind was now in a totally different space. My joy had been stolen from me with those four simple words: "I want a divorce." After my pastor prayed for me, he encouraged me to attend the leadership meeting, as I needed to be surrounded by my believing friends.

The second phone call I made was to my friend in Toronto. I had been staying with her throughout the *100 Huntley Street* experience. We had known each other for many years and had come through many similar Christian character-building experiences. She had been there for me during these past few very exciting days and I needed her to be with me now. I needed her to pray. The enemy was mounting a serious attack on my marriage and I knew that intercessory prayers from my closest friends would ensure victory.

The third phone call was to another close friend, one who lived nearby and was also a powerful intercessor. I shared with her what had just happened and asked that she pray for me and Jim and our marriage.

Over the next few days, I discovered that Jim had premeditated this decision. He had had the house appraised while I was away. He knew what it was worth and how much would be available to each of us when the house was sold. He was already starting to look for another place to live. Everything was planned out. There was no room for discussion and no need for counselling.

Finally, after much begging, he agreed to postpone everything for three weeks. In his mind, he was doing this to allow me to accept the inevitable. He was leaving and our marriage was over. However, in my mind, I took this delay as a time to devote myself to some serious prayer and fasting.

For twenty-one days, I sought God, prayed, cried, and asked God to intervene. There was absolutely no way the enemy was going to rob me and my family of what God intended. My three intercessory prayer partners joined in spiritual warfare with me. I believed for a miracle. I was standing upon the promises of God. By my declaration of faith, everything was going to work together for the good. This next season would be difficult, as I was prepared to make many compromises to ensure our marriage remained intact. I would do whatever it took to ensure Jim didn't leave our home.

Well, guess what? At the end of the twenty-one days, Jim informed me that nothing had changed. The house was going up for sale and he was leaving at the end of August (which was in a couple of weeks). I said that there was absolutely no way I would allow our family home to be sold. Over the next several hours, I begged, pleaded, and cried on my knees in front of him not to do this to our family. I would do whatever was required to keep this marriage intact. Although I knew that it would be difficult for me to change in the natural, God would give me the grace and strength to walk through whatever was ahead.

Well, at the end of the conversation, after many tears and boxes of tissues, Jim agreed to not sell the home. Instead of using his portion of the equity to buy a home for himself, he would rent for the next six months. However, during this time, he would be looking for a property to purchase and advised me to start getting my personal finances in order. In other words, get my own bank account, my own credit card, and start to accept the fact that we were no longer a couple.

I barely remember the balance of that night except that I sat cuddled up in the fetal position on one of our living room chairs, crying out to God. How could this be happening? I had already walked through one divorce prior to becoming a believer. How, as a spirit-filled Christian with God on my side, could I be asked to walk through another split? What would my family think? What kind of witness would this be? What about our thirteen-year-old son? This was the worst possible time in his life for something like this. What about my future speaking engagements? What about promoting my book? What about my leadership role in my church? Everything was falling down around me.

Then the negotiations with God began. Although my season of prayer and fasting hadn't resulted in the outcome I had been praying for, I began to ask God if He would intervene in other ways.

One summer afternoon, I went swimming in the lake behind our home. The cool water was refreshing compared to the blazing summer sun. It wasn't long before I realized that these cool afternoon swims would soon become a memory of times gone by. If God didn't intervene, by this time next year Jim and I would be living apart, on our way to divorce court with many of our matrimonial possessions sold. This home would be one of them.

"God, why can you not work in Jim and me while we're still living together?" I asked. "Why does this event have to be so public, with such an impact on our family? Why does our youngest son have to witness this painful division?"

When Jim and I had first been married, God had placed us in the same canoe till death do us part. Why could God not fix us while we were both in the same canoe?

Then God said that Jim needed to be in his own canoe. Okay, I reasoned, God wants to do a work in each of us separately. Then I asked God, "Why can you not keep our canoes at least tied together? That would keep us separate but also together. Can you not do your work without this significant separation?"

I was then given a powerful rebuke from God. "Do you not trust Me? You believe that you need Jim's canoe tied to yours so you can witness My hand at work. Do you think you need to supervise My work to ensure that I do it correctly? What if I choose to take Jim's canoe in a different direction? What if I choose to lead Jim's canoe around the island out of your sight and have Jim stop at a different shore? Do you not trust Me?"

Wow! Was I still operating in that much control? Even though I said I trusted God, there appeared to be conditions placed upon that trust. I only trusted God when I could see with my own eyes what God was doing. Now I was being asked to trust God even when I couldn't physically see what God was doing.

Over the next few weeks, with fresh tears continually falling from my eyes, I was numb. Walking though the routine of each day was all I could handle. The façade. The pain. Then, a week after we celebrated our son Brandon's thirteenth birthday, Jim moved out with almost half our furnishings. Jim and I had agreed that I would take Brandon out for the day, which included a pancake breakfast, attending a movie of his choice, and then a hike along our favourite Elbow Falls pathway. During these few hours, Jim and his buddy moved everything out. Jim said that he would be at home when we returned so he could personally tell Brandon what was happening. I will never forget my son's agonizing screams as he crumpled to the floor, watching his dad carry the last few things from our family home. Brandon watched me sit ghost-like in one of our living room armchairs, drinking a cup of herbal tea with tears running down my cheeks. He could see the depths of my agony and was insistent that his dad give me a hug and kiss as he said goodbye. As if this simple action would make everything better and the reality of the situation would go away...

What can I say? The next few months were the most difficult I have ever faced in my Christian walk. After sharing this with the leadership team at church and my co-workers, I also had to advise two pastors who had requested that I speak at their churches later that September. Eventually, everyone had to know what was happening. I think the hardest part of all was when I met casual friends and acquaintances and they asked how my interview at *100 Huntley Street* had gone. I couldn't even respond, because in my mind that was no longer a memorable event. Much more memorable was the fact that upon my return, on the way home from the airport, my husband had asked for a divorce. I couldn't even share this tragic news. I was simply too ashamed.

I remember standing at my kitchen sink, crying out to God, "How could this have happened? God, I don't understand." I would barely start the sentence and God would interrupt me, saying, "Barbara, I did not ask you to understand. I asked you to trust me."

"Ahh! God, how do I do that?" Everything in the natural cried out for justice. I was fighting my tendency to be angry... to be bitter.... to manipulate the situation to get him back. Then I would move on to stubbornness, thinking, "I'll show you. I'll change the locks on the doors. I'll burn everything that belongs to you. I'll move away and you will never see your son again." Yet in my spirit, I knew that I knew that I knew that I was not to lean on my own understanding. I was to trust in the Lord with all my heart.

That's how the theme of this book was conceived. During the following months, as I continued to cry out to God, He showed me how to trust Him. Was it easy? Certainly not. However, what became easier every day was my acceptance that trusting God is better than being in control and reacting my own way.

GROUP DISCUSSION
Share with the group a traumatic personal situation when you stopped paddling and trusted God. What were the results?

HOW DO YOU LEARN HOW TO TRUST? | 3

Through the past two chapters, we have studied many scriptures in the Bible which reveal what God's word says about trust. These scriptures have stated what will happen when we choose to trust Him. In addition, other verses show us what will happen when we choose not to trust God.

If we reflect on the following scriptures, we are told how to trust God (with all our heart) and when to trust God (at all times).

Trust in the Lord with all your heart and lean not on your own understanding; In all your ways acknowledge him, and he will make your paths straight. (Proverbs 3:5–6)

Trust in him at all times, O people; pour out your hearts to him, for God is our refuge. (Psalm 62:8)

1. TRUST MEANS ACCEPTING DISCIPLINE

In your struggle against sin, you have not yet resisted to the point of shedding your blood. And you have forgotten that word of encouragement that addresses you as sons: "My son, do not make light of the Lord's discipline, and do not lose heart when he rebukes you, because the Lord disciplines those he loves, and he punishes everyone he accepts as a son." (Hebrews 12:4–6)

When life deals us a curve ball, trusting with our hearts becomes very difficult and the "at all times" part becomes impossible for us to do in the natural. When our situations are difficult, we must understand that we may have created the circumstances ourselves, through choices we made. As a result, God may be using this season to discipline us.

Think back upon your earthly parents. When you did something wrong and you were disciplined, did you cry out, "I don't trust you any more"? I suspect not. If you were like me, you may have cried out, "I don't love you anymore." But shortly afterwards, you would have been running up to your father to say that you were sorry and that you really did love him very much. If you understood and accepted then that earthly discipline happens out of love, why do we now interpret God's discipline as a consequence of not trusting? Nothing could be further from the truth. If we love God and trust Him, we must accept it when God needs to discipline us.

2. TRUST IS THE OPPOSITE OF CONTROL

It is for freedom that Christ has set us free. Stand firm, then, and do not let yourselves be burdened again by a yoke of slavery... So I say, live by the Spirit, and you will not gratify the desires of the sinful nature. For the sinful nature desires what is contrary to the Spirit, and the Spirit what is contrary to the sinful nature. They are in conflict with each other, so that you do not do what you want. But if you are led by the Spirit, you are not under law. The acts of the sinful nature are obvious: sexual immorality, impurity and debauchery; idolatry and witchcraft; hatred, discord, jealousy, fits of rage, selfish ambition, dissensions, factions and envy; drunkenness, orgies, and the like. I warn you, as I did before, that those who live like this will not inherit the kingdom of God. But the fruit of the Spirit is love, joy, peace, patience, kindness, goodness, faithfulness, gentleness and self-control. Against such things there is no law. Those who belong to Christ Jesus have crucified the sinful nature with its passions and desires. Since we live by the Spirit, let us keep in step with the Spirit. Let us not become conceited, provoking and envying each other. (Galatians 5:1, 16–26)

When we don't trust God, we gratify our sinful nature and choose to operate out of a sense of control. We may become sexually immoral and impure. We may keep our focus on false gods or rely on horoscopes for decision-making. We may become subject to hating our neighbours, being jealous of our siblings, and having angry outbursts for the slightest offence. We may become ambitious, wanting the corner office and expecting promotions and rewards even when we haven't earned them. Through our words, we may cause doubt and division. Through our attitudes, we may be seen as impatient, insensitive, and superficial. Through our actions, we may be deemed to be uncaring, selfish, and full of pride.

When we trust God and live by the Spirit, we will be rewarded with the fruit of the Spirit. Instead of control, people will see love, joy, peace, patience, kindness, goodness, faithfulness, gentleness, and self-control in our lives.

3. LEARNING TO TRUST

I would like you to reflect for a moment on those early days—the days after you first got saved. Remember the day you got saved and asked Jesus into your heart, the day you first stepped into the canoe and left shore. Remember those early years when you were learning who Jesus was and why He died for you. You loved relaxing with Him in the canoe, reading His word, and learning the sound of His voice. Even remember the many times in your Christian journey when you found it easy to not paddle your canoe.

Salvation gets you into the canoe.
Relationship helps you stay in the canoe.
Trust shows you *when* to paddle your canoe.

Before we learn to trust God—and I mean *really* trust God, not something that merely looks like we trust God—we need to spend some time reflecting on our own personal canoe journey. For example, when you first accepted Jesus into your heart as your Lord and Saviour, you stepped into the canoe. When you got into the canoe that day, where did you sit? Where we sit when we first got in the canoe depends upon the conditions in our lives leading up to our salvation. Where we sit will also depend upon how much baggage we bring into the canoe with us. Did you accept Jesus into your heart when you were very young, in your teen years, or as an adult? Was it a decision made out of your broken emotions or was your decision made as a result of your intellectual pursuit of truth?

For example, if you were saved when you were very young, you would find it easy to step into the canoe and move toward the back where your Father is sitting with the paddles. You would likely sit very close to your Father, maybe even on His knee. You would find safety and comfort feeling Him so close.

If you accepted Jesus into your heart when you were a young adult and had just come out of a season of rebellion, you probably carried some of life's baggage into the canoe with you. You may have chosen to abandon your lifestyle and leave some of your baggage on the shore. However, it's probable that you still managed to bring a lot of baggage into the canoe with you. Given the weight of this baggage and the amount of space it takes up, you would either place it in the middle of the boat, where you could see it, or continue to carry it on your back (like a large knapsack). In either case, you would be forced to sit near the front of the canoe. There's no way you could sit near the back because your weight would tip the canoe over.

If you accepted Jesus into your life much later in life—as a mature adult—there may not have been a lot of baggage. At least, not that you were aware of. Your life's journey and the wisdom and counsel you obtained along the way may have helped you to deal with a lot of your baggage. However, given how long you walked without Jesus, it's likely you still got into the front of the canoe. Why? Your knowledge of physics would tell you not to put too much weight in the back, which would cause the front end to tip up. Psychology would lead you to be independent and you wouldn't deem it necessary to use God as a crutch. You could handle the front of the canoe. There seems to be a sense of being in control when you're in the front. Or possibly, it was an emotional decision—one based on fear. Perhaps you remember how your earthly father treated you and you suspect it would be safer to sit further away from your heavenly Father. Perhaps you want to be out of reach of His rod of discipline, just in case He's thinking about punishing you for all the things you did before you got into the canoe.

Scriptures for Reflection
Where did you first learn to trust the Father?

1. Up Front and Facing Front
   a) Fear
      - *"Fear the Lord your God, [and] serve him..."* (Deuteronomy 6:13)
      - *"Serve the Lord with fear..."* (Psalm 2:11)
      - *"I will show you whom you should fear..."* (Luke 12:5)

   _____

   _____

   _____

   _____

   b) Freedom
      - *"...to proclaim freedom for the captives..."* (Isaiah 61:1)
      - *"...you have set my heart free"* (Psalm 119:32).
      - *"...the truth will set you free"* (John 8:32).

   _____

   _____

   _____

   _____

2. Middle and Facing Front
   a) Security and Safety
      - *"...you have made my lot secure"* (Psalm 16:5).
      - *"...an anchor for the soul, firm and secure"* (Hebrew 6:19).
      - *"...he will keep me safe in his dwelling"* (Psalm 27:5).

   _____

   _____

   _____

   _____

b) Stability and Steadfastness
- *"By justice a king gives a country stability..."* (Proverbs 29:4)
- *"It is for freedom that Chris has set us free. Stand firm, then, and do not let yourselves be burdened again by a yoke of slavery"* (Galatians 5:1).

_____

_____

_____

_____

3. Middle and Facing Back
   a) Learning His Character
   - *"A father to the fatherless, a defender..."* (Psalm 68:5)
   - *"As a father has compassion..."* (Psalm 103:13)
   - *"I will be a Father to you..."* (2 Corinthians 6:18)

_____

_____

_____

   b) Keeping You from Temptation
   - *"Our Father in heaven... lead us not into temptation..."* (Matthew 6:9, 13)
   - *"And God is faithful; he will not let you be tempted beyond what you can bear. But when you are tempted, he will also provide a way out so that you can stand up under it"* (1 Corinthians 10:13).
   - *"...you will protect me from trouble..."* (Psalm 32:7)

_____

_____

_____

_____

4. At the Back
   a) Father-heart (on his lap)
   • *"And by him we cry, 'Abba Father'"* (Romans 8:15).
   • *"I will be Father to you, and you will be my sons and daughters, says the Lord Almighty"* (2 Corinthians 6:18),
   • *"If you then, though you are evil, know how to give good gifts to your children, how much more will your Father in heaven give the Holy Spirit to those who ask him!"* (Luke 11:13)

_____

MY STORY

Salvation got me into the canoe.
Relationship kept me in the canoe.
Trust taught me *not* to paddle my canoe.

If you're practical and analytical like me, you want to know what mature trust looks like. I'm not talking about the posture of trust you demonstrated when you first got saved and got into the canoe. I'm not talking about the next level of trust you gained when you were getting to know Jesus and He was actually teaching you how and when to paddle. I'm talking about the trust that's required when the storms of life come your way and Jesus tells you not to paddle at all, those times when everything in the natural tells you to take control.

How was I going to trust God despite my circumstances? Once again, I was about to become a single mother. How was I going to trust God in my relationships? I was soon to be a twice-divorced woman. How was I going to tell my family, parents, and business colleagues? How could I be in a place of leadership in the church with this shameful event in my life? Remember, I was the one who had labelled it shameful. At no time did God say that my situation was shameful!

"God, how do I trust you?" I asked. "Does trust mean that I stand still? Does it mean that I do nothing? Or does it mean that I aggressively proceed, with a 'just in case You don't show up' attitude?"

I learned that trusting God has a posture, and in this current situation, God had a specific posture for me to take. What was that posture? Was I to passively wait with an attitude of tranquil prayer? Was I to retreat to a safe place—a shelter, a haven—away from all the shame? Was I to become aggressive? Was this the time for serious spiritual warfare? I had been engaged in spiritual warfare for over a month and my husband had still moved out. What about being assertive? In other words, were there any practical actions I could take? Was there something in my life God wanted to deal with? Were there things I should have been doing that would bring hope and encouragement? What was the difference, anyway?

GROUP DISCUSSION

Imagine if this was your story. How would you react if you took one of the following postures? Would you still want to paddle and be in control, or would you choose not to paddle and trust God?

Reflect upon the following postures. First, what would it mean in the context of the world in which we live? Then, what would it mean when we chose to trust God? I have started to fill in the chart on the next page. Which words would you add?

POSTURE	CONTROL	TRUST
Passive	Envy Jealousy	
Retreat	Bitterness Anger	
Aggressive	Spiteful I'll show you	
Assertive		
In the Fire		
Hidden		
Forgotten		

Esther Becomes Queen

But after Xerxes' anger had subsided, he began thinking about Vashti and what she had done and the decree he had made. So his personal attendants suggested, "Let us search the empire to find beautiful young virgins for the king. Let the king appoint agents in each province to bring these beautiful young women into the royal harem at the fortress of Susa. Hegai, the king's eunuch in charge of the harem, will see that they are all given beauty treatments. After that, the young woman who most pleases the king will be made queen instead of Vashti." This advice was very appealing to the king, so he put the plan into effect.

At that time there was a Jewish man in the fortress of Susa whose name was Mordecai son of Jair. He was from the tribe of Benjamin and was a descendant of Kish and Shimei. His family had been among those who, with King Jehoiachin of Judah, had been exiled from Jerusalem to Babylon by King Nebuchadnezzar. This man had a very beautiful and lovely young cousin, Hadassah, who was also called Esther. When her father and mother died, Mordecai adopted her into his family and raised her as his own daughter.

As a result of the king's decree, Esther, along with many other young women, was brought to the king's harem at the fortress of Susa and placed in Hegai's care. Hegai was very impressed with Esther and treated her kindly. He quickly ordered a special menu for her and provided her with beauty treatments. He also assigned her seven maids specially chosen from the king's palace, and he moved her and her maids into the best place in the harem.

Esther had not told anyone of her nationality and family background, because Mordecai had directed her not to do so. Every day Mordecai would take a walk near the courtyard of the harem to find out about Esther and what was happening to her.

Before each young woman was taken to the king's bed, she was given the prescribed twelve months of beauty treatments—six months with oil of myrrh, followed by six months with special perfumes and ointments. When it was time for her to go to the king's palace, she was given her choice of whatever clothing or jewelry she wanted to take from the harem. That evening she was taken to the king's private rooms, and the next morning she was brought to the second harem, where the king's wives lived. There she would be under the care of Shaashgaz, the king's eunuch in charge of the concubines. She would never go to the king again unless he had especially enjoyed her and requested her by name.

Esther was the daughter of Abihail, who was Mordecai's uncle. (Mordecai had adopted his younger cousin Esther.) When it was Esther's turn to go to the king, she accepted the advice of Hegai, the eunuch in charge of the harem. She asked for nothing except what he suggested, and she was admired by everyone who saw her.

Esther was taken to King Xerxes at the royal palace in early winter of the seventh year of his reign. And the king loved Esther more than any of the other young women. He was so delighted with her that he set the royal crown on her head and declared her queen instead of Vashti. To celebrate the occasion, he gave a great banquet in Esther's honor for all his nobles and officials, declaring a public holiday for the provinces and giving generous gifts to everyone.

*Even after all the young women had been transferred to the
second harem and Mordecai had become a palace official, Esther
continued to keep her family background and nationality a secret.
She was still following Mordecai's directions, just as she did when
she lived in his home.*

Mordecai's Loyalty to the King

*One day as Mordecai was on duty at the king's gate, two of the
king's eunuchs, Bigthana and Teresh—who were guards at the door
of the king's private quarters—became angry at King Xerxes and
plotted to assassinate him. But Mordecai heard about the plot and
gave the information to Queen Esther. She then told the king about
it and gave Mordecai credit for the report. When an investigation
was made and Mordecai's story was found to be true, the two men
were impaled on a sharpened pole. This was all recorded in* The
Book of the History of King Xerxes' Reign.

Haman's Plot against the Jews

*Some time later King Xerxes promoted Haman son of
Hammedatha the Agagite over all the other nobles, making him the
most powerful official in the empire. All the king's officials would
bow down before Haman to show him respect whenever he passed
by, for so the king had commanded. But Mordecai refused to bow
down or show him respect.*

*Then the palace officials at the king's gate asked Mordecai,
"Why are you disobeying the king's command?" They spoke to him
day after day, but still he refused to comply with the order. So they
spoke to Haman about this to see if he would tolerate Mordecai's
conduct, since Mordecai had told them he was a Jew.*

*When Haman saw that Mordecai would not bow down
or show him respect, he was filled with rage. He had learned of
Mordecai's nationality, so he decided it was not enough to lay hands
on Mordecai alone. Instead, he looked for a way to destroy all the
Jews throughout the entire empire of Xerxes.*

So in the month of April,* during the twelfth year of King Xerxes' reign, lots were cast in Haman's presence (the lots were called purim) to determine the best day and month to take action. And the day selected was March 7, nearly a year later.

Then Haman approached King Xerxes and said, "There is a certain race of people scattered through all the provinces of your empire who keep themselves separate from everyone else. Their laws are different from those of any other people, and they refuse to obey the laws of the king. So it is not in the king's interest to let them live. If it please the king, issue a decree that they be destroyed, and I will give 10,000 large sacks of silver to the government administrators to be deposited in the royal treasury."

The king agreed, confirming his decision by removing his signet ring from his finger and giving it to Haman son of Hammedatha the Agagite, the enemy of the Jews. The king said, "The money and the people are both yours to do with as you see fit."

So on April 17 the king's secretaries were summoned, and a decree was written exactly as Haman dictated. It was sent to the king's highest officers, the governors of the respective provinces, and the nobles of each province in their own scripts and languages. The decree was written in the name of King Xerxes and sealed with the king's signet ring. Dispatches were sent by swift messengers into all the provinces of the empire, giving the order that all Jews— young and old, including women and children—must be killed, slaughtered, and annihilated on a single day. This was scheduled to happen on March 7 of the next year. The property of the Jews would be given to those who killed them.

A copy of this decree was to be issued as law in every province and proclaimed to all peoples, so that they would be ready to do their duty on the appointed day. At the king's command, the decree went out by swift messengers, and it was also proclaimed in the fortress of Susa. Then the king and Haman sat down to drink, but the city of Susa fell into confusion.

Mordecai Requests Esther's Help

When Mordecai learned about all that had been done, he tore his clothes, put on burlap and ashes, and went out into the city, crying with a loud and bitter wail. He went as far as the gate of the palace, for no one was allowed to enter the palace gate while wearing clothes of mourning. And as news of the king's decree reached all the provinces, there was great mourning among the Jews. They fasted, wept, and wailed, and many people lay in burlap and ashes.

When Queen Esther's maids and eunuchs came and told her about Mordecai, she was deeply distressed. She sent clothing to him to replace the burlap, but he refused it. Then Esther sent for Hathach, one of the king's eunuchs who had been appointed as her attendant. She ordered him to go to Mordecai and find out what was troubling him and why he was in mourning. So Hathach went out to Mordecai in the square in front of the palace gate.

Mordecai told him the whole story, including the exact amount of money Haman had promised to pay into the royal treasury for the destruction of the Jews. Mordecai gave Hathach a copy of the decree issued in Susa that called for the death of all Jews. He asked Hathach to show it to Esther and explain the situation to her. He also asked Hathach to direct her to go to the king to beg for mercy and plead for her people. So Hathach returned to Esther with Mordecai's message.

Then Esther told Hathach to go back and relay this message to Mordecai: "All the king's officials and even the people in the provinces know that anyone who appears before the king in his inner court without being invited is doomed to die unless the king holds out his gold scepter. And the king has not called for me to come to him for thirty days." So Hathach* gave Esther's message to Mordecai.

Mordecai sent this reply to Esther: "Don't think for a moment that because you're in the palace you will escape when all other Jews are killed. If you keep quiet at a time like this, deliverance and relief for the Jews will arise from some other place, but you and your relatives will die. Who knows if perhaps you were made queen for just such a time as this?"

41

Then Esther sent this reply to Mordecai: "Go and gather together all the Jews of Susa and fast for me. Do not eat or drink for three days, night or day. My maids and I will do the same. And then, though it is against the law, I will go in to see the king. If I must die, I must die." So Mordecai went away and did everything as Esther had ordered him. (Esther 2:1–4:17, NLT)

King Xerxes, during a time of celebration and under the influence of much wine, ordered his queen to appear before the assembled princes. When the queen refused, the king took the advice of his wise men, dethroned her, and sent her away. After a kingdom-wide search for a new queen, several young women—one of whom was Esther, a Jew—were chosen to be prepared for presentation to the king. After twelve months of preparation, Esther, who had kept her heritage secret, was presented to the king. He was pleased with her beauty and made her his new queen.

Despite her position, Esther aligned herself with the Jewish people and their customs. When she heard that Naham, the Chief Counsel for the king, was planning a total annihilation of her people, she fasted and prayed for three days. She stood in the gap, preparing to meet with the king, at which time she could present her request that the decision to kill all the Jewish people be overturned.

Esther wasn't afraid of the consequences of requesting a meeting with the king without first being summoned. Because of her trust in God, she said, "If I must die, I must die." In other words, the result of her actions was in God's hands and not the king's. Because of her preparation, which included her and all those around her fasting, the king granted her request. Do not think that her trust in God came as a result of three simple days of fasting. Her trust in God had been nurtured over her entire time in the king's palace.

Esther is often commended and recognized for her heroism and self-denial. Rather than being self-centred and remaining hidden in her identity as the queen, she exposed who she was and became willing to suffer the same potential consequences as every other person of her faith.

I often dwell upon the previous twelve months, during which Esther undertook a series of preparations before being presented to the king. She had six months of oil of myrrh and six months of perfumes and cosmetics. She was hidden in a harem with many other women, all of whom were going thought the same treatments. I suspect it was a very competitive environment. I liken it to a beauty pageant, with each young woman competing to win the crown—or in this case, the favour of the king. Esther probably wasn't caught up in lobbying for position. She lived in a place of obedience, doing exactly as she was told. She honoured all who were given authority over her. As a result, she won the favour of many of those entrusted to care for her.

Why six months of oil of myrrh? Was one month not long enough? What is myrrh? There must have been many other oils that could have been used. *Commipihora myrrha*, which we refer to as myrrh, has a rich, smoky balsamic aroma that is purifying, restorative, revitalizing, and uplifting. It is a helpful aid to meditation, having one of the highest levels of sesquiterpenes available. Sesquiterpenes are a class of compounds having a direct effect on our amygdale, the seat of our emotions. Wow! Not only was the oil's aroma revitalizing, restorative, and uplifting, but it had a direct effect on Esther's emotions. To draw a comparison, she had the opportunity to experience six months of emotional healing. How many books have been written about how to heal our damaged emotions? According to the book of Esther, all we need is six months in a spiritual spa being administered the oil of myrrh.

Myrrh has a litany of health benefits beyond that of healing our emotions. It is an antiviral that won't let microbes grow or infect you. Myrrh is an astringent that contracts the skin and muscles. It is an expectorant that relieves congestion. In addition to having antifungal properties, it also stimulates blood circulation and stimulates our brains and nervous systems. Myrrh is a diaphoretic, which means it increases sweats and keeps us free from toxins and excess water in our body. It is an antiseptic as well as an immunity booster. Myrrh benefits the circulatory system, operates as a tonic, and also is an anti-inflammatory. Do I need to go on? I think we would all welcome the opportunity to have six months of oil of myrrh treatments.

After these six months, can you imagine another six months of beauty treatments? We're not talking about a new haircut, manicure, and pedicure. Esther had six months of attention given to her outer beauty. Six months! It's not like she needed to heal from a facelift. She was still a young woman with no wrinkles or crow's feet around her eyes. She would have had no frown lines or age spots on her skin from being in the sun too long.

Why would she need six months? I have concluded that these six months weren't just about cosmetics and beauty treatments. I believe it was about patience. She needed to be comfortable with not understanding all the reasons. She only had to understand that she needed to trust God. When you know you're being presented to the king after six wonderful months enjoying the benefits of the oil of myrrh, you might conclude that a week is all you'd need to get your hair, nails, and face done. Would you be willing to wait another twenty-five weeks before being presented to the king? Compare this to your preparations for your wedding day. After doing all you know to do in preparation for the big day, how would you feel to be asked to wait with your bridesmaids almost six months before your dream is fulfilled?

After Esther became queen, she was known for her patriotism. She honoured those in authority over her. That she obeyed every instruction that came from her Uncle Mordechi proves she was willing to be obedient. Finally, she was an intercessor. She was willing to stand in the gap for people who couldn't stand up for themselves.

Because Esther was neither manipulative nor thought herself superior to others, the story has an amazing ending. Her preparation, patience, and persistence paid off. Haman, the enemy in this story, was killed and the Jewish people were allowed to live in spiritual freedom. What did God reward her with for her willingness to submit to all the beauty treatments, time of preparation, and honouring of her elders? She was given the king of Persia.

We can pull many illustrations from Esther's story. With respect to how we as women should be living our lives today, we could say that we are not to be selfish. We are to be heroic and unafraid to stand in the gap, standing up against injustice. We should not deny our heritage. We should honour those around us. We should be intercessors. Most importantly, we should allow God to prepare us for His purpose. We should be willing to go through seasons of waiting and preparation—spiritual spas—so that we're prepared for the tasks God sets before us.

Do you deny yourself in order to stand in the gap for others? Do you fast and pray so the bonds of injustice can be broken? Are you an advocate for the poor, the widow, the orphan, the refugee? Do you seek opportunities to assist those who aren't as privileged as yourself? Esther could have denied her heritage and embraced all that a life of royalty entailed. Instead she sacrificed everything—her identity, and potentially even her life, in order to stand in the gap.

Wherever your sphere of influence is—work, community, school, or family—let your light shine. Let your conduct and attitude be a positive influence to those around you. God will give you favour.

If willing, God will bring you through seasons of spiritual renewal (spas) so that He can use you in a strategic time and place.

MY STORY

After Jim left, I read the story of Esther often. I asked, "God, are you telling me that I'm entering a season that may last twelve months? Are you telling me that I need emotional healing—a spiritual spa?"

I began to take an inventory of myself. Yes, I still had lots of flaws. I certainly needed more emotional healing! Although God had healed me of many damaged emotions and tragedies in my life, I could certainly allow Him to go deeper. Now that Jim wasn't around, God could bring me through these healings in a more private manner. I welcomed the oil of myrrh into my life.

"Holy Spirit, I surrender all," I prayed. "Create in me a clean heart. Restore to me the joy of my salvation.

Nothing was going to be out of bounds. I really did want to be that Proverbs 31 woman of gentle and quiet spirit. I wanted to submit and honour the man of God who had been given to me as my husband. Although I may not have been seeing the fruit in Jim's life, I needed to trust God.

I began to understand that the situation I was in wasn't just about Jim and his journey to redemption. God was taking me on a journey as well. I embraced this season, albeit not willingly at first. What were some of the characteristic flaws in me God wanted to address?

To aid myself in the process, I chose to become accountable. I met with my pastor and his wife on a regular basis. I regularly attended church meetings and times of corporate prayer. I prayed with friends and I prayed on my own. I even sought out a Christian psychiatrist for counselling. Why did I voluntarily do all these things? I needed to know that if Jim didn't come back, it wasn't because of me. I wanted to do everything in my power and ability. I would even have let God keep me hidden so that when the time for our reunion came, Jim would be presented with a better, more spiritually refined wife than when he had left our marriage.

Scriptures for Reflection

…she was given the prescribed twelve months of beauty treatments… (Esther 2:12, NLT)

_____

_____

_____

_____

_____

_____

_____

…she was admired by everyone who saw her. (Esther 2:15, NLT)

_____

_____

_____

_____

_____

_____

…fast for me. Do not eat or drink… If I must die, I must die. (Esther 4:16, NLT)

_____

_____

_____

_____

_____

_____

_____

PERSONAL LEADERSHIP EXAMPLE

Have you been in a workplace setting where you felt like God had hidden you? Has there been a time in your career when you knew God was going deeper in your life, teaching you to trust Him as He developed patience and perseverance in your character? A time when you knew you weren't supposed to paddle? A time when you had no ambition or need to be in control?

In my lengthy career as a leader in the not-for-profit world, I fondly recall my five-year stint as the financial administrator for a children's rehabilitation centre outside Toronto. I was a baby Christian, only saved for about eighteen months. God had provided me with a wonderful position in an esteemed organization that was less than twenty minutes from where I lived. The executive director was one of the best bosses I've ever had. She became a mentor in my life. She demonstrated the type of female leader I aspired to be. This was a safe place. As a result, God was able to focus on my spiritual health. Week after week, one weekend retreat after another, God worked in my life. He was healing me, restoring me, and building in me the attributes of Esther. I was letting that oil of myrrh perform its miraculous work in my life.

This wasn't the time to be assertive or aggressive. Neither was this a posture of passivity or retreat. This was a posture of trusting God while He had me hidden. I didn't aspire to promotions, increased responsibilities, or more authority. I was content with where God had placed me for this season in my life. Although I had no idea how long this season would last, I knew God would eventually open the cocoon and allow me to break free.

This would be one of the many stops along the way toward my ultimate destiny. While here, God began to show me what it meant to be a woman of God in leadership. He led me to study the attributes of not only Esther, but also Deborah, Ruth, Abigail, and Mary. God used this workplace setting to weave into my life the characteristics of a female leader who would trust God as she counselled others, served others, interceded for others, provided for others, and rested in her knowledge and understanding of who she was in Christ.

GROUP DISCUSSION

Has there been a time when you knew God had hidden you for a season? Did you try to break out prematurely? Did you patiently wait for Him to release you? What did your spiritual spa look like? How was the oil of myrrh used in your situation?

HOW DO YOU TRUST?
IN THE LION'S DEN

5

Daniel in the Den of Lions

It pleased Darius to appoint 120 satraps to rule throughout the kingdom, with three administrators over them, one of whom was Daniel. The satraps were made accountable to them so that the king might not suffer loss. Now Daniel so distinguished himself among the administrators and the satraps by his exceptional qualities that the king planned to set him over the whole kingdom. At this, the administrators and the satraps tried to find grounds for charges against Daniel in his conduct of government affairs, but they were unable to do so. They could find no corruption in him, because he was trustworthy and neither corrupt nor negligent. Finally these men said, "We will never find any basis for charges against this man Daniel unless it has something to do with the law of his God."

So the administrators and the satraps went as a group to the king and said: "O King Darius, live forever! The royal administrators, prefects, satraps, advisers and governors have all agreed that the king should issue an edict and enforce the decree that anyone who prays to any god or man during the next thirty days, except to you, O king, shall be thrown into the lions' den. Now, O king, issue the decree and put it in writing so that it cannot be altered—in accordance with the laws of the Medes and Persians, which cannot be repealed." So King Darius put the decree in writing.

Now when Daniel learned that the decree had been published, he went home to his upstairs room where the windows opened toward Jerusalem. Three times a day he got down on his knees and prayed, giving thanks to his God, just as he had done before. Then these men went as a group and found Daniel praying and asking God for help. So they went to the king and spoke to him about his royal decree: "Did you not publish a decree that during the next thirty days anyone who prays to any god or man except to you, O king, would be thrown into the lions' den?"

The king answered, "The decree stands—in accordance with the laws of the Medes and Persians, which cannot be repealed."

Then they said to the king, "Daniel, who is one of the exiles from Judah, pays no attention to you, O king, or to the decree you put in writing. He still prays three times a day." When the king heard this, he was greatly distressed; he was determined to rescue Daniel and made every effort until sundown to save him.

Then the men went as a group to the king and said to him, "Remember, O king, that according to the law of the Medes and Persians no decree or edict that the king issues can be changed."

So the king gave the order, and they brought Daniel and threw him into the lions' den. The king said to Daniel, "May your God, whom you serve continually, rescue you!"

A stone was brought and placed over the mouth of the den, and the king sealed it with his own signet ring and with the rings of his nobles, so that Daniel's situation might not be changed. Then the king returned to his palace and spent the night without eating and without any entertainment being brought to him. And he could not sleep.

At the first light of dawn, the king got up and hurried to the lions' den. When he came near the den, he called to Daniel in an anguished voice, "Daniel, servant of the living God, has your God, whom you serve continually, been able to rescue you from the lions?"

Daniel answered, "O king, live forever! My God sent his angel, and he shut the mouths of the lions. They have not hurt me, because I was found innocent in his sight. Nor have I ever done any wrong before you, O king."

The king was overjoyed and gave orders to lift Daniel out of the den. And when Daniel was lifted from the den, no wound was found on him, because he had trusted in his God.

At the king's command, the men who had falsely accused Daniel were brought in and thrown into the lions' den, along with their wives and children. And before they reached the floor of the den, the lions overpowered them and crushed all their bones.

Then King Darius wrote to all the peoples, nations and men of every language throughout the land: "May you prosper greatly! I issue a decree that in every part of my kingdom people must fear and reverence the God of Daniel. For he is the living God and he endures forever; his kingdom will not be destroyed, his dominion will never end. He rescues and he saves; he performs signs and wonders in the heavens and on the earth. He has rescued Daniel from the power of the lions."

So Daniel prospered during the reign of Darius and the reign of Cyrus the Persian. (Daniel 6:1–28)

This story takes place around 580 B.C., after the destruction of Jerusalem by the Babylonians. All of the citizens, including Daniel, a young man at the time, were taken captive by King Nebuchadnezzar to live in Babylon. Daniel, along with his friends Shadrach, Meshach, and Abednego, found favour with the king and were given positions of influence. Despite their unwillingness to bow down to idols and their choice to worship God, they continued to be given great power and authority—all because they trusted God.

After the death of Nebuchadnezzar, his son Belshazzar became king. Although he had witnessed the conversion of his father to faith in God, he chose to set himself up against God. In addition, he took Daniel and his friends out of leadership positions, so they were no longer operating in any advisory capacity to the king.

Belshazzar's reign lasted only a short time before the Babylonians were invaded by the Medes, under the leadership of King Darius. We don't know the reason Darius chose the people he did for leadership positions. Possibly all the previous leaders were killed during the invasion. All we know is that Daniel was appointed as one of three main administrators over the 120 satraps in the kingdom. In modern-day terminology, this would be similar to being the Premier of a province or Governor of a state.

We could conclude that Daniel once again became successful. Although his career under two previous kings had ranged from leadership to rejection, he now found himself in one of the highest possible positions in regional government. As a result of his constant and unwavering trust in God, combined with his proven knowledge and wisdom, God rewarded him and placed him in a position of honour, influence, and authority.

As with any political environment, Daniel had adversaries. The leaders of the "opposition" parties were doing everything they could to discredit Daniel. No matter what they tried, nothing worked. Rather than discrediting Daniel, they watched as King Darius arranged to increase Daniel's authority to that of ruler over the kingdom.

Daniel was about to be named Prime Minister or President of the country. His adversaries were unsuccessful in finding any form of corruption or negligence in Daniel, as he was a man beyond reproach. They concluded that the only way to find a basis for charges against Daniel would be if it had something to do with the law of God.

These men, after gaining the support of the majority of representatives in all the regions, approached the king to bring in a new law. Similar to a new bill being introduced to legislature, these men brought forward their petition.

As we read in the story, they were successful in their plot. For thirty days, no one could pray to any god or man, unless it was King Darius. They even legislated the penalty for breaking the law. Those found guilty would be thrown into the lion's den.

Knowing this law had passed, why did Daniel not choose to continue his prayer times in private? Isn't that what we would do? If we were living in a country that forbade us to practice our Christian beliefs, would we not continue to do so privately? We would meet with other believers in secret places. We would hide our Bibles. We certainly wouldn't be found praying in public places, nor would we be found praying in front of open windows where people could see and hear us.

Yet Daniel didn't hide his faith. As a result of his trust in God, he continued to bow down and worship God three times a day, right in front of his window, knowing his adversaries would hear him and report him. Daniel knew the penalty for being found guilty of this crime. He knew he would be caught and thrown into the lion's den—a death sentence.

Daniel wasn't afraid of a death sentence. However, this wasn't a death by firing squad or electrocution. This wasn't going to be an instant death. This would be a potentially slow and painful death by not one lion, but by several very hungry lions.

Place yourself in this situation. Would you be that courageous? Would you be able to trust God so much so that you could face the hungry beasts in the lion's den? How powerful a position of trust is that, of being able to trust God even though it means death? How surprised would you be when the lions only walked around you and never laid a paw on you? Would you be confident that God would send His angel to shut the mouths of the lions? Would you believe the lions wouldn't hurt you because you were innocent in God's sight and had not done anything wrong to dishonour the earthly king?

What a testimony of trust! What a reward for this trust! Have you ever been in a place of leadership where you were at the hands of adversaries who wrongfully accused you? Did your situation result in court hearings or prison sentences? I liken it to being in front of "twelve angry men" set on your destruction. Were you able to choose to not pick up the paddles and defend yourself? Did you allow God to defend you? What did it look like? What was the outcome?

MY STORY

In my marriage, were there times when I was falsely accused of something I hadn't done? Was there a situation where I had to rely on God to defend me? After reflecting upon the past twenty years of life with Jim, I can honestly say that I was never faced with this situation.

In other relationships, yes! There have been times when I was wrongfully accused. There have been times when I had to rely on God to defend me. I've had to walk away from these accusations and leave justice and vengeance in the hands of God. Was it easy? Not at all! By making deliberate and difficult choices, I had to put my trust in God and rely on His ways, not mine. I knew God's ways were higher than my ways. I knew His purposes were higher than my purposes. I knew that all things work together for good for those who are called to His purpose. I may not have understood why I was falsely accused, but I did understand that at some point everything would turn to the good.

I have never had to face any form of undeserving punishment that would have resulted in me being locked away or cast aside. The "lions" I have faced in my Christian journey have come in the form of false accusations and abandonment from friends—one of whom was one of my bridesmaids, to whom I am still not reconciled. The lions have come in the form of hardships and challenges on the mission field. The lions have come in the form of satanic attacks during my sleep—all of which were overcome by praying the blood of Jesus.

Have you been falsely accused of having an affair? Has your husband or wife filed for divorce because they honestly believed the lies people around them were telling them?

Scriptures for Reflection

They could find no corruption in him, because he was trustworthy and neither corrupt nor negligent. (Daniel 6:4)

_____

_____

_____

_____

_____

_____

When he came near the den, he called to Daniel in an anguished voice, "Daniel, servant of the living God, has your God, whom you serve continually, been able to rescue you from the lions?" (Daniel 6:20)

_____

_____

_____

_____

_____

_____

And when Daniel was lifted from the den, no wound was found on him, because he had trusted in his God. (Daniel 6:23)

_____

_____

_____

_____

_____

_____

PERSONAL LEADERSHIP EXAMPLE

Although I've never been in any parliamentary or political roles, I've been on the board of directors in three different organizations. When I reflect upon each of these organizations, I cannot think of any situations where I have been falsely accused. I cannot think of individuals who may have been jealous of my position and tried to get me removed. I was never deemed a threat to anyone I served with.

However, there was one organization where I worked in a contractual arrangement rather than as an employee. I travelled across Canada as one of their corporate trainers, providing one-day workshops on such topics as administration, customer service, and leadership. At the end of each workshop, I would ask the participants to complete an evaluation of the session with respect to the materials that were covered, as well as my ability to facilitate learning. How effective had the day been? Had they learned anything? Would they recommend this session to someone else? Would they attend another of my workshops in the future?

Without meaning to brag, in every single workshop my average rating was four out of five. Never did I receive any rating below three. Although a few individuals would give me an average score, the majority of attendees always stated that the day had exceeded their expectations. I suspect that when my scores were tabulated at the organization, there were differing opinions on whether I should be given more work or be considered a threat to others on contract presenting the same materials.

I had hoped the evaluations would result in me receiving more assignments and being asked to give more workshops on progressively more difficult materials. I had already proven I could achieve the same results whether I was teaching an inexperienced group of administrative assistants or mature leaders in corporate Toronto. Instead I was brought into the office and accused of a series of seemingly insignificant actions. Apparently, I had been rude to their receptionist. I was accused of being too impatient when I came to pick up my materials only to learn that the box wasn't ready as they had promised. I was accused of being insensitive, and as a result they would no longer require my services.

Yes, that's right! Other facilitators who had been there longer felt threatened. They had concluded that I would be getting more assignments and they would get fewer. Their income was threatened, not to mention their self-esteem.

After leaving the office that day, devastated by what had been said and shocked by their decision, my self-esteem took a significant blow. Maybe I really wasn't a good facilitator. Maybe I was rude and insensitive. This was hard to believe, considering every previous subordinate and workplace peer had told me the exact opposite. It wasn't until several months later that I learned every Christian who had worked for that organization had been released from their service. Now it all began to make sense. I hadn't been released as a result of their petty reasons; I had been dismissed because of my faith. My co-workers were being convicted by the presence of God whenever I was around them.

You'll never guess how God intervened. Not long afterwards, less than a year, the company went bankrupt. All I could say was, "Thank you, God, for removing me from that situation before it got messy." I had been fully paid for all my work. I was now too far removed to be associated with any misdealings or corruptions. We could conclude that because of how they treated the Christians in their midst, God caused their company not to prosper.

GROUP DISCUSSION
Share a situation with the group when you were wrongfully accused. Were you fired from your job or "packaged out" for reasons that could not be defended? Have you ever served in a governing or political role? Were you able to not paddle and trust God?

HOW DO YOU TRUST? PASSIVE | 6

Elisha: Known as a Prophet

Elisha Traps Blinded Arameans
Now the king of Aram was at war with Israel. After conferring with his officers, he said, "I will set up my camp in such and such a place."
The man of God sent word to the king of Israel: "Beware of passing that place, because the Arameans are going down there."
So the king of Israel checked on the place indicated by the man of God. Time and again Elisha warned the king, so that he was on his guard in such places.
This enraged the king of Aram. He summoned his officers and demanded of them, "Will you not tell me which of us is on the side of the king of Israel?"
"None of us, my lord the king," said one of his officers, "but Elisha, the prophet who is in Israel, tells the king of Israel the very words you speak in your bedroom."
"Go, find out where he is," the king ordered, "so I can send men and capture him." The report came back: "He is in Dothan." Then he sent horses and chariots and a strong force there. They went by night and surrounded the city.

When the servant of the man of God got up and went out early the next morning, an army with horses and chariots had surrounded the city. "Oh, my lord, what shall we do?" the servant asked.

"Don't be afraid," the prophet answered. "Those who are with us are more than those who are with them."

And Elisha prayed, "O Lord, open his eyes so he may see." Then the Lord opened the servant's eyes, and he looked and saw the hills full of horses and chariots of fire all around Elisha.

As the enemy came down toward him, Elisha prayed to the Lord, "Strike these people with blindness." So he struck them with blindness, as Elisha had asked. (2 Kings 6:8–18)

In this Old Testament story, we have an account of how the prophet Elisha trusted God. Elisha didn't fear the Aramean army that was at war with Israel. As a matter of fact, God was using Elisha to warn the king of Israel where the armies of Aram were going to be. Time and time again, the king of Israel was prepared for what the king of Aram was planning. As a result, the Arameans were getting very upset. The king of Aram was convinced there was a spy in the midst of his camp. When he questioned his advisors, he was told that the prophet Elisha was prophetically telling the king of Israel everything the king of Aram was sharing in the secrecy of his own bedroom. Finally, knowing who the spy was and where he would be, the king of Aram went to Dothan to capture Elisha.

Now, if Elisha was so prophetic, he would have known that the king of Aram was coming. But this time he didn't warn anybody, not the king of Israel and not even his own servant. I suspect Elisha knew when he awoke in the morning that the city of Dothan would be surrounded by the enemy. Elisha didn't rally the king of Israel to mount an attack. He simply said to his personal servant, who I suspect was anxious, fearing for his life that day, "Those who are with us are more than those who are with them." Now, that's trust, knowing that more are the forces with you than those who are in the world! He was confident in the God he served and knew that he knew that he knew that the victory would be theirs that day. He didn't lift a finger. He didn't change his posture at all.

He simply prayed that God would strike the enemy with blindness. And that's exactly what God did.

Can you imagine what that would have done for your faith if you had been Elisha's servant? Having witnessed Elisha share prophetic words of strategic warfare with the king of Israel on a regular basis, you would have wondered what had happened. Why didn't Elisha provide the king of Israel with advance warning? Had he lost his touch? Or would you have believed that this was the day destined for you to die? Instead, the servant witnessed something that increased his own personal faith and trust in God. I would speculate that Elisha didn't warn anyone of what was going to occur because he wanted the king of Israel and his armies, the king of Aram and his armies, his personal servant, and all the citizens of Dothan to know that they served the Almighty God.

Just imagine that you were one of the watchmen on the wall of Dothan. During the night, the enemy had secretly surrounded the city without uttering a sound. When the light of dawn appeared over the horizon, you and all your comrades would have sounded the alarm: "We are surrounded. Everyone to their battle posts. Get your weapons, and when the commanding officer gives the signal, be prepared to fight!" Then, much like our visibility increases when the morning mist evaporates, you would see that there was another army coming down the hills behind the Arameans. The enemy would not be able to retreat. Instead, this eastern facing army, riding on white horses with silver helmets protecting their heads, silver breastplates protecting their bodies, and large silver shields by their sides would be caught in the light of the rising sun.

In the natural, this would have been how the enemy was blinded and sent into confusion. However, this wasn't in the natural. When the morning fog dissipated, all the citizens of Dothan saw the enemy around their city. Only when Elisha prayed did they see the angelic hosts. What an amazing sight that would have been!

MY STORY

As I was journeying through this season in my life, once again as a single working mother, I began to ask God to strengthen me with His word.

I was beginning to understand that God wanted me to trust Him by doing nothing. No more pleading, no more begging, no more phone calls, and certainly no drives by Jim's new place of residence.

As I asked God to show me how to trust Him like Elisha had trusted, God began to give me scripture passages I could lean into. He gave me promises and insights into the purposes of His word. He showed me the struggles and victories of the patriarchs of the Old Testament, such as the times when Abraham and Isaac were passive. He showed me how the apostles of the New Testament had trusted God, even though they knew they would be persecuted.

It wasn't long before God gave me a passage that revealed what He was doing in my husband's life. As a result, I called this season "Operation Peniel." God had given me a strategy on how I could pray not just for strength for myself, but also for strength for my estranged husband.

Jacob Wrestles with God

That night Jacob got up and took his two wives, his two maidservants and his eleven sons and crossed the ford of the Jabbok. After he had sent them across the stream, he sent over all his possessions. So Jacob was left alone, and a man wrestled with him till daybreak. When the man saw that he could not overpower him, he touched the socket of Jacob's hip so that his hip was wrenched as he wrestled with the man. Then the man said, "Let me go, for it is daybreak." But Jacob replied, "I will not let you go unless you bless me." The man asked him, "What is your name?" "Jacob," he answered. Then the man said, "Your name will no longer be Jacob, but Israel, because you have struggled with God and with men and have overcome."

Jacob said, "Please tell me your name." But he replied, "Why do you ask my name?" Then he blessed him there.

So Jacob called the place Peniel, saying, "It is because I saw God face to face, and yet my life was spared." The sun rose above him as he passed Peniel, and he was limping because of his hip. (Genesis 32:22–31)

When I read this story of Jacob, who was later renamed Israel, I began to understand what God was doing with Jim. This was Jim's "Peniel." This would be the place where Jim would wrestle with God. In the end, however long it took, God would win. When God won and Jim surrendered, God would give him a new name and a new purpose. Jim would eventually cross his river of isolation and rejoin his family.

I realized that in Jacob's story, the wrestling match only lasted one night. I fully understood that in Jim's case it may take much longer. All I had to do was take the same posture as Elisha. I needed to remain passive and wait on my side of the river until Jim rejoined me and his family so we could continue our journey together.

Scriptures for Reflection

"Don't be afraid," the prophet answered. "Those who are with us are more than those who are with them." (2 Kings 6:16)

_____

_____

_____

_____

_____

_____

_____

_____

...but those who hope in the Lord will renew their strength. (Isaiah 40:31)

_____

_____

_____

_____

_____

_____

_____

In the morning, O Lord, you hear my voice; in the morning I lay my requests before you and wait *in expectation.* (Psalm 5:3, emphasis added)

_____

_____

_____

_____

_____

PERSONAL LEADERSHIP EXAMPLE

Example 1. I have had examples of this posture in my own life. The first was a situation where I knew God was telling me to be still. I was not to retreat and I was not to confront.

Most of my employment situations have taken me one step beyond what I was comfortable handling, which meant I had to rely on the strength and wisdom of Jesus to get me through each day. In one particular company, I had a very demanding, domineering, and controlling boss. No matter what I did, he would redo it. Since he was a perfectionist, I soon discovered that he would recheck everything I did. No matter how hard I tried, he always found something to correct.

My self-esteem and confidence decreased rapidly. Restless Sunday nights would become anxious Monday mornings. I decided that, for sanity's sake, I needed to take some control of my life and find other employment. Given my credentials, it wasn't long before I got an interview for a comparable position a little closer to home. However, when the job offer came, I didn't have that overwhelming feeling of joy. I was hesitant and couldn't understand why. I had wanted out of my current company and had found another job, so why didn't I have any peace about moving on?

Through the aid of prayer and reading devotionals, the Lord led me through some of Paul's journeys. One of his voyages in particular ministered to me. In Acts 27, Paul was a prisoner on a ship bound for Rome. The captain of the ship was advised to winter in a place called Fairhaven. However, he refused to listen. Instead, the ship continued on its journey, got caught in a strong storm, and shipwrecked on the island of Malta. None of the crew or prisoners were lost through this ordeal. After waiting for better weather, they continued on to Rome and Paul arrived there safely.

This passage ministered to me immensely. You see, no matter which course was taken, no matter whether they wintered in Fairhaven or Malta, Paul would still have arrived at his destination. The Lord had said that it would be better if Paul and company wintered in Fairhaven.

Similar to Elisha's posture, God was telling me to do nothing. God wanted me to trust in Him—to be still and know that He was God. It was better for me to be passive and winter in Fairhaven than venture out into new territory. God didn't only teach me how to lead with patience and perseverance; He showed me how to trust Him completely in this difficult situation.

In the end, I stayed with the company for almost five years. By continuing to trust God under the leadership of this controlling individual, God began to open doors for me to witness, not only to the general manager but also to many co-workers who couldn't understand why I would put up with my boss. God had another purpose. He needed me to passively trust Him in this workplace setting so that His ultimate purpose could be achieved. As a result, God used me as a light to many people who have since become fellow believers in Jesus Christ.

Example 2. In another situation, I was with an organization for one short season—barely a year. To the natural eye, it may have appeared that I was simply taking up space and not accomplishing much. Why was I even there? My job offer had stated I was to develop a strategic resource development plan for the registered charity, and I knew I would be able to lead my staff through that process.

However, resource development wasn't my passion. I knew the theory of the role and I knew the results that could be achieved if we followed best practices. That year, through my calmness, perceived passivity, and the encouragement I provided my co-workers, my team succeeded in raising more money in one Christmas season than the organization had ever raised before. I had stood still, not lifted a paddle, and God moved miraculously.

There may not have been an angelic host hovering over the building, but there was certainly a Holy Spirit fragrance wherever I set my foot. God let His light shine through me so the people around me saw not only my good works, but the glory of the Father. God used me to encourage my co-workers in their Christian walks. He used me to pray for colleagues who were ill. He used me to draw the backslidden closer to His bosom. He used me to provoke a curiosity to the unsaved. God used me as His Elisha.

GROUP DISCUSSION

Share a situation when, without any warning, the enemy had you surrounded. What did you do? Did you sound the battle cry? Did you run and hide within the safety of your walls? Did you stand and cry out, "Those who are with me are more than those who are with them"? Were you able to sit passively, fully confident in your trust in God that the victory would be yours?

HOW DO YOU TRUST? PASSIVE

7

Mary: Known as a Worshipper

At the Home of Martha and Mary

As Jesus and his disciples were on their way, he came to a village where a woman named Martha opened her home to him. She had a sister called Mary, who sat at the Lord's feet listening to what he said. But Martha was distracted by all the preparations that had to be made. She came to him and asked, "Lord, don't you care that my sister has left me to do the work by myself? Tell her to help me!"

"Martha, Martha," the Lord answered, "you are worried and upset about many things, but only one thing is needed. Mary has chosen what is better, and it will not be taken away from her." (Luke 10:38–42)

Jesus Comforts the Sisters of Lazarus

On his arrival, Jesus found that Lazarus had already been in the tomb for four days. Bethany was less than two miles from Jerusalem, and many Jews had come to Martha and Mary to comfort them in the loss of their brother. When Martha heard that Jesus was coming, she went out to meet him, but Mary stayed at home.

*"Lord," Martha said to Jesus, "if you had been here, my brother
would not have died. But I know that even now God will give you
whatever you ask."*

Jesus said to her, "Your brother will rise again."

*Martha answered, "I know he will rise again in the resurrection
at the last day."*

*Jesus said to her, "I am the resurrection and the life. He who
believes in me will live, even though he dies; and whoever lives and
believes in me will never die. Do you believe this?"*

*"Yes, Lord," she told him, "I believe that you are the Christ, the
Son of God, who was to come into the world."*

*And after she had said this, she went back and called her sister
Mary aside. "The Teacher is here," she said, "and is asking for you."
When Mary heard this, she got up quickly and went to him. Now
Jesus had not yet entered the village, but was still at the place where
Martha had met him. When the Jews who had been with Mary
in the house, comforting her, noticed how quickly she got up and
went out, they followed her, supposing she was going to the tomb to
mourn there.*

*When Mary reached the place where Jesus was and saw him,
she fell at his feet and said, "Lord, if you had been here, my brother
would not have died." (John 11:17–32)*

Mary and Martha were sisters who lived in the village of
Bethany, which was two miles outside Jerusalem. They and
their brother Lazarus had become disciples of Jesus Christ
and were known to have a close relationship with Him. We know this
because whenever Jesus and His disciples were in the area, they would
stay at their home. Martha was always distracted with preparations,
preoccupied with providing the best hospitality for her guests. On the
other hand, Mary always chose to sit at Jesus' feet and listen to His
teachings.

Does this mean Mary was so spiritual that she was of no earthly
good? Does this indicate that Mary was lazy, not wanting to help her
sister in the domestic chores? Was Mary selfish, not wanting to share

Jesus with her sister? Did she want Him all to herself? Was Mary oblivious or indifferent to everything and everyone around her? In fact, nothing could be further from the truth. Mary was a woman who chose what was better. Jesus said that what she had chosen would not be taken away from her.

When you review the passage from John 11, we learn of how Mary and Martha acted when Jesus arrived four days after the death of their brother Lazarus. When they learned that Jesus had arrived, Martha ran out to meet Him. Yet Mary stayed home.

When I first read this passage, I was a bit puzzled. Knowing the relationship Mary had with Jesus, I would have expected her to be the one running to meet Him and wanting to be comforted. I would have expected Martha to be busy hosting the many Jews who had come to comfort them. Yet it was Martha who went while Mary stayed behind. Had their roles reversed? Knowing that Mary had previously chosen that which was better, was Martha now the one wanting to be with Jesus? We learn that Mary was resting, because the scripture states that when Martha came back and told her that Jesus was asking for her, she got up quickly. In other words, it wasn't until Jesus asked for her that she got up and went to meet him.

The key word in both of these passages is "resting." When we're in a passive posture, we aren't distracted. Instead we're at rest. We aren't anxious to find the answers. We patiently wait for God's plans to be unveiled. We rest in God's timing, knowing that His ways will prevail, not our ways. Jesus could have healed Lazarus before he died. Jesus could have come and raised Lazarus from his mourning bed after he died and before he was buried. Bethany wasn't a long walk from Jerusalem. It was only two miles! Instead Jesus waited until Lazarus had been in the tomb for four days.

Mary knew Jesus could have healed Lazarus at any time, because she had already seen Him heal Lazarus of leprosy. She saw no need to anxiously run out to Jesus to express her concern or seek to be comforted. Because of her relationship with him, she knew that although she may not understand what was happening, her sorrow would be comforted. She trusted Jesus.

When we contemplate what a passive posture of trust looks like, we may conclude some of the following:

- Someone who rests on God's word.
- Someone who is of quiet concern.
- Someone who is submissive.
- Someone who "knows" God because they have spent time with Him.
- Someone who is a worshipper.

Today, many of us find ourselves becoming Marthas. As wives and mothers, we're constantly aware of the needs and concerns of our households and families. Amidst the demands of meal preparation, ensuring our homes are clean, and extending hospitality to those God brings our way, we may forget that which is better. Not that we are to neglect our duties, but that we shouldn't neglect that which should be first—spending time with God.

In other words, we should spend time at the feet of Jesus before we become involved in our daily tasks. If we first choose Jesus and spend time with Him in His word and in His presence, the other duties we are to accomplish will not be done begrudgingly.

I cannot stress enough how important it is for us to spend time with God every morning. By reading God's word, meditating on passages of scriptures, and spending time in prayer, we are able to face the day without anxiety or stress. How many of you know that this is often the most difficult thing to do? That extra fifteen minutes of sleep is so welcoming.

It's important that we not be anxious. Instead, we are to be of "quiet concern." We know and trust that God's ways are not our ways. God will reveal His purpose in His time. We need to *rest*. As the first few chapters of the book of Hebrews states, we are to "wrestle" to enter that rest. That means it's not a posture that comes easy. We must actively pursue it.

MY STORY

When Jim left our marriage, I wrestled to enter that position of rest. I could have lost myself in the busyness of life by working longer days, volunteering for more activities, and constantly being around other people. Being quiet and sitting at the feet of Jesus wasn't an easy posture for me. Remember, I'm a woman who's prone to depression, so not being busy could trigger another deep, dark season in my life. It would have been easy for me to choose to hide in my dark bedroom, trying to comfort myself with boxes of chocolates.

Instead I chose to rest in God's word. That meant reading my Bible even when I didn't feel like it. It meant going to church when I didn't feel like it. It meant being around other believers when I didn't feel like it. It meant I had to choose that which was better. All of these activities are better than watching non-redemptive television programs, reading silly love stories, or getting lost at work by spending more time with a multitude of unbelievers.

In addition, this meant I couldn't run after Jim. I couldn't go over to his new home, pounding on the door and begging to talk to him. Instead I had to exercise this posture of passive trust—by doing nothing. No overt actions. No anxiousness. I had to wait.

Scriptures for Reflection

...who sat at the Lord's feet listening to what he said. (Luke 10:39)

_____

_____

_____

_____

_____

_____

_____

...has chosen what is better... (Luke 10:42)

_____

_____

_____

_____

_____

_____

This is what the Sovereign Lord, the Holy We of Israel, says: "In repentance and rest is your salvation, in quietness and trust is your strength, but you would have none of it. (Isaiah 30:15)

_____

_____

_____

_____

_____

_____

PERSONAL LEADERSHIP EXAMPLE

I'd been working for a faith-based medical mission. Becoming involved with this ministry during its birthing years meant I was the only one able to handle many of the administrative tasks. With a mandate to keep the Canadian overhead below ten percent of total revenues, our office was often manned by only me and a few volunteers. On many occasions, when there was work to be done, I had to step up to the plate. Many weeks, I put in endless hours as the Martha of the workplace. With a never-ending list of things to do, it was difficult to become a Mary in my position with Jesus.

I was simply too busy to take time to pray. I bet you can guess what happens to us when we start to get imbalanced like that. He'll create situations so difficult that the only way we can work through the challenges is to pray—not by might, not by power, but by the spirit of the Lord. In other words, it isn't what we do or plan that brings victory. It isn't that well-written glossy newsletter that brings in hundreds of donations. It isn't that classy black-tie banquet that results in a major gift. It isn't a state-of-the-art website with Facebook, Twitter, YouTube, and goodness knows what other buttons that help to increase the donor base.

God has showed me time and time again that my excessive "Martha" efforts often get in the way of God performing a miracle. For example, at one point, we were in an extreme cashflow situation. I had no idea where the money was going to come from in order for us to make the payroll obligations the following week, let alone process the mid-month funds transfer to Malawi. I was doing everything in my power. I was making phone calls, sending letters, e-mails, everything in the natural that I knew to do. Then I decided to sacrificially give of my own consulting company's earnings. I made a significant matching donation in order to leverage other donations that were coming in. That way, the medical work in Malawi could continue.

Well, one evening during praise and worship in church, Holy Spirit began to speak to me. "Barb, you have prevented God from performing a miracle."

"What do you mean?" I asked.

Let's say that you're a little girl and your mommy has just bought you a brand new pretty dress. When your daddy comes home from work, he wants you to put on the dress and model it for him in the living room. He wants you to do that little twirl thing you do in ballerina class. Instead you tell your daddy that you don't have time to dance for him that night. You have an entire carton of boxed chocolate almonds that need to be sold for your dance class's fundraiser. You need to go door-to-door in your neighbourhood in order to sell them all.

Now, don't get me wrong. There's nothing wrong with what you want to do. However, with a wink of His eye, your father could arrange for all those almonds to be sold. In other words, if you had chosen to dance before your daddy that evening, he would have been so pleased with his little girl that he would have said, "Honey, why don't you give me that cartoon of almonds? I can sell them to the guys at work tomorrow. Plus, it'll give me a chance to let them know that my little girl is training to be a ballerina and that she has a dance recital in a couple of weeks. It will give me the opportunity to invite each of them and their families to see you perform."

Do you understand what I'm saying? By being a Martha, we can actually get in the way of what God wants to do. His ways are not our ways. He sees the big picture when we don't. Is there a situation in your life where you find it difficult to be passive? Can you sit quietly like a Mary? Can you giggle and dance before the Lord in an attitude of worship? Can you forget all the lists that are sitting on the kitchen counter? Remember, if we delight in the Lord, He will give us the desires of our heart. With a snap of His finger, God can miraculously lay it on someone's heart to do exactly what you need done. So, rest awhile! Be still and know that He is God.

GROUP DISCUSSION

As a group, take a moment to be quiet. When you empty your minds of all the day's trials and tomorrow's challenges, do you hear God's voice? What is He saying? What scripture is being repeated in your mind?

HOW DO YOU TRUST? RETREAT

8

David: Known as a Man After God's Own Heart

David Flees

A messenger came and told David, "The hearts of the men of Israel are with Absalom."

Then David said to all his officials who were with him in Jerusalem, "Come! We must flee, or none of us will escape from Absalom. We must leave immediately, or he will move quickly to overtake us and bring ruin upon us and put the city to the sword."

The king's officials answered him, "Your servants are ready to do whatever our lord the king chooses."

The king set out, with his entire household following him; but he left ten concubines to take care of the palace. So the king set out, with all the people following him, and they halted at a place some distance away. All his men marched past him, along with all the Kerethites and Pelethites; and all the six hundred Gittites who had accompanied him from Gath marched before the king.

The king said to Ittai the Gittite, "Why should you come along with us? Go back and stay with King Absalom. You are a foreigner, an exile from your homeland. You came only yesterday. And today shall I make you wander about with us, when I do not know where I am going? Go back, and take your countrymen. May kindness and faithfulness be with you."

But Ittai replied to the king, "As surely as the Lord lives, and as my lord the king lives, wherever my lord the king may be, whether it means life or death, there will your servant be."

David said to Ittai, "Go ahead, march on." So Ittai the Gittite marched on with all his men and the families that were with him.

The whole countryside wept aloud as all the people passed by. The king also crossed the Kidron Valley, and all the people moved on toward the desert.

Zadok was there, too, and all the Levites who were with him were carrying the ark of the covenant of God. They set down the ark of God, and Abiathar offered sacrifices until all the people had finished leaving the city. (2 Samuel 15:13–24)

One of the toughest postures to take when we are trusting God is the posture of retreat. How can we trust God if we're running away? In this story, King David has been reigning over Israel for many years. Throughout his life, he has trusted God. He trusted God as a young shepherd boy when the lion or bear came after his sheep. It was more than skill and courage that brought about the death of the predator; it was David's trust in God.

This is the same David who killed Goliath. As a result of seeing God rescue him from the paw of the lion, David knew God would rescue him from the hand of this Philistine. David said that this uncircumcised Philistine would be like one of the animals he had killed. After all, this foreigner had defied the armies of the living God.

This is the same David who played the harp for King Saul, knowing Saul was given to demonic oppression—so much oppression that Saul actually threw a spear at David. Did David run away? No. He knew he was to stay and comfort his king.

However, now we see this mighty King David, who had seen God deliver him from wild animals. He had seen God deliver him from Goliath. He had seen God deliver him from King Saul. Why would he not think God would deliver him from his son Absalom's attack on Jerusalem? Surely King David, who possessed "a heart after God's own heart," could trust God to save him and his household without them having to flee.

Because of David's sin, he may have thought God would no longer protect him. David was guilty of killing Uriah, the husband of Bathsheba, when he learned that Bathsheba was pregnant as a result of a night of passion with King David. David was a murderer and adulterer. Although the prophet Nathan confronted David and David confessed of his sin and repented, did he think God was no longer "with him"? Had he really accepted God's forgiveness?

Knowing who King David was, despite his sin and shortcomings, we know he trusted God. By reading the book of Psalms, we know David trusted God in all circumstances—in good times and bad, in times of family sickness and in times of health, in poverty when he lived in caves and in riches when he lived in the palace with all his wives and concubines, in times of celebration and in times of mourning. Therefore, we conclude that he trusted God in his current circumstance as well.

David didn't retreat from Jerusalem because he was afraid and felt God had abandoned him. He left Jerusalem because God told him to leave. If David had been afraid, he may have slipped away in the night. Instead he left the city during the day with a large procession that included family, friends, supporters, visiting dignitaries, and his entire council. The priests and prophets left with him. Why? Because he was taking the Ark of the Covenant. This meant he was taking God with him. Remember, in the Old Testament, before God's word became flesh, God's presence was in the Ark of the Covenant.

David was honoured as he left Jerusalem. The citizens of the city witnessed this event and wept as the members of David's household passed. Everyone knew and understood that David's decision to retreat meant their ultimate safety would be assured. David knew that if he and his family stayed in Jerusalem, Absalom would bring ruin upon them and put the citizens of the city to the sword.

MY STORY

During our separation, there were times when I had to choose a posture of retreat. What did I retreat from? In the previous chapter, I referred to wanting to hide in my bedroom. That could have been an illustration for retreat. However, it wouldn't have been a healthy retreat. A healthy retreat is when we deliberately take a step back.

I chose to retreat from ministry. Although I had a few speaking engagements lined up, I needed to seek God to determine if I was to retreat from those commitments. I could have elected to not say anything to these other church leaders. I could have simply shown up on the designated dates and shared my message from my book. I could have prayed with people at the altar and then quietly returned home. However, that would have been very deceptive, and in some ways hypocritical. I had to choose to face my circumstances, bury any shame and guilt I was feeling, and let these pastors know what was happening in my life. I could not fear their judgment for my situation.

Just like David couldn't fear man's judgment for leaving Jerusalem, I couldn't fear man's judgment by cancelling speaking engagements. Don't think this was easy for me to do. Being a type-A personality, the decision was difficult to back away and say, "No, I cannot and should not do this." I had finally reached a pinnacle in ministry (or so I thought), only to learn that I needed to back away. This wasn't the time to move ahead. This was a time to move back.

Scriptures for Reflection

Then David said to all his officials who were with him in Jerusalem, "Come! We must flee, or none of us will escape from Absalom." (2 Samuel 15:14)

_____

_____

_____

_____

_____

_____

You made us retreat before the enemy... (Psalm 44:10)

_____

_____

_____

_____

_____

When they had gone, an angel of the Lord appeared to Joseph in a dream. "Get up," he said, "take the child and his mother and escape to Egypt. Stay there until I tell you, for Herod is going to search for the child to kill him." (Matthew 2:13)

_____

_____

_____

_____

_____

_____

PERSONAL LEADERSHIP EXAMPLE

Several years ago, I had the opportunity to be part of a steering committee whose mandate was to investigate the feasibility of starting a new Christian school in our city. Initially, the school would offer only Kindergarten through Grade Six. However, the intent was to increase by one grade each year, with the eventuality that students could continue in this faith-based learning environment through Grade Twelve.

The feasibility study was successful and we began the process of starting the new school. Through miraculous provision, we were able to purchase an old public school building. During the planning stages, the steering committee became the initial school council. Given that we were being partially financed through our local church, this council had a reporting relationship to the church's board of governors, as well as to the school superintendent.

When the school officially opened, I fulfilled a dual role. I was both the treasurer of the school's advisory council and a consultant to the founding president. My mandate was to get their financial systems installed, establish financial protocols, and put in place the required accounting procedures. I was also requested to provide leadership and training to the office staff.

A year into the assignment, I began to struggle with some ethical dilemmas as they related to my profession. I'm a professional accountant and thus am required to abide by our associations' code of ethics and professional conduct. Although we were a Christian organization, established with faith-based governing principles, some employee conduct issues and operational practices were beginning to occur that weren't God-honouring or biblically based.

To some, my professional standards may have appeared to be too high. However, given that I also had to align myself to God's standards, I deemed that these standards represented the principles I needed to abide by. Yes, we operated in grace, mercy, and forgiveness. However, we also needed to operate with discipline, truth, honour, and respect for God's word.

Everything came to a head when I was asked to push the creative envelope of accounting further than I was comfortable with regarding donations and employee benefits. When my concerns were ignored or deemed unfounded, I realized that I had to defer to my professional code of conduct and make a decision.

As a point of reference, I've taken the liberty of inserting an excerpt from this code of conduct (*Certified Management Accountants of Alberta - Code of Ethics*) below and personally highlighting the words that had the greatest influence on how I operated.

As professionals, CMAs are governed by a rigorous Code of Ethics and Professional Conduct that demands they carry out professional work with *honesty, impartiality, courtesy and personal honor*. The relationship between a member of the Society of Management Accountants, other members of the Society of Management Accountants, other professionals, and members of the public must be governed by certain standards of professional and ethical conduct. These standards govern the performance of a member's duties, to ensure that those duties are discharged in accordance with acceptable accounting and management practices, *and a high level of professional integrity*.

It is the duty of every member of the Society to uphold and foster the competence and prestige of the accounting profession. In keeping with the Society's high standards of conduct, members must carry out their professional work with *honesty, impartiality, courtesy and personal honour*. A breach of the Principles of Conduct outlined below will constitute professional misconduct and will render the offending member liable to such disciplinary measures that the Society may consider appropriate.

A professional approach to an ethical problem requires that the rules be treated as setting out the minimum standard of behaviour, not the maximum. Where the rules are silent, an even greater sense of responsibility is called for to ensure the course of action followed reflects the general standards that have been established by members of the Society over the years.

As a result, I had to resign from my positions and direct involvement with the school. In other words, God was asking me to retreat—to back away rather than try to obtain justice. That would need to be God's role. Was it easy to back away? No. Was it easy to not see justice served? No. However, it became obvious over time that not all battles are mine to fight. Some belong only to the Lord. In other words,

God, help me to accept the things I cannot change,
the ability to change the things I can,
and the wisdom to know the difference.

Of note, when I finally made the decision to remove myself from the situation, believing God had closed a door, another opportunity presented itself. In other words, God opened a window.

The window God opened was the role of manager of finance and administration for a large Calgary tourist attraction. It was an amazing place to work. My fellow managers were excellent. Those in leadership roles—such as the general manager, community members on the various committees, and the directors on the board—knew and understood the vision, mission, and mandate of the organization and took their roles very seriously.

Added to this environment of professional competence and integrity was a complement of passionate volunteers, as well as regular and seasonal staff who enjoyed being part of an opportunity to bring western Canadian history alive to all who visited this forty-acre park along the banks of the Glenmore reservoir.

In my mind, I had found the perfect job. I had a position of responsibility that utilized my professional skills. I had an amazing boss and great co-workers. I was earning a decent salary and only had to commute twenty minutes each way for work. The organization was respected and had won many tourism awards. Plus, I had an amazing west-facing view from my office; I could see the entire park against the backdrop of the Canadian Rocky Mountains. I thought to myself, "This is where I'll work for the rest of my career. No more five-year stints. I'll be here until I retire."

Initially, I was responsible for the accounting, information technology, warehouse operations, administration, and human resources. When the general manager went on a medical disability leave, I was asked to assume the leadership of food services as well. For the next twelve months, the managers of the organization, of which I was one, were tasked with co-managing the facility without any formal leadership in place. How that year unfolded is another story onto itself and one I will not dwell upon.

When it was learned that our general manager's medical leave would be longer than originally anticipated, an assistant manager was hired. Shortly thereafter, we went through a reorganization exercise and created a three-member executive management team which included this assistant general manager, a chief operating officer, and a chief financial officer. I was asked to assume the role of CFO, so additional middle managers began to report to me. At one point, I used to joke that "everything that breathed" reported to me, including the horses!

My days were varied, exciting, and challenging. In addition to providing leadership to areas I was comfortable operating in, I was responsible for retail operations, historical operations (which included agriculture and the horses), and guest services. With the exception of those who were responsible for the infrastructure of the park—such as transportation, grounds, housekeeping, and capital projects—everyone reported to me in some manner. At one point, over 1,500 employees were under my authority.

In my mind, this was the absolute pinnacle of my career. I was at the point of "self-actualization" that is often referred to in Maslow's Theory of Human Motivation. I was at the place of knowing my full potential and realizing it. I had a desire to accomplish everything I could and become the most I could be.

Well, God had other plans! It turned out that this wasn't to be the last spot on my canoe journey. God began to nudge me that it was time to get back into the canoe. I asked "Why? And where am I going?" God simply told me to trust Him. Unfortunately, I wasn't immediately willing to obey. As a result, God had to change my situation so that I would leave.

Through a series of circumstances, it soon became apparent that I couldn't continue to work with the new assistant manager. In our private discussions, I would provide counsel against making certain decisions, only to hear after the fact, in a public forum, that he was inferring that I was in perfect alignment with where he was leading the organization. He was misrepresenting me and making me out to be a hypocritical fool to my staff and subordinates. My attempts to confront him were laughed off as me being too sensitive. When I approached his supervising authority (the board of governors), I soon realized that it was his word against mine.

Although it was the furthest thing from the truth, I was painted as a manager who was spurned by initially not being offered this man's position. I knew I would lose the battle, so once again I needed to back away. There were some things I couldn't change. It was time to retreat.

Where would I go? What would I do next? This time, the retreat resulted in me taking a sabbatical from the workforce entirely. This season would include me writing my first book, improving my public speaking skills, and volunteering within the community.

When God tells us to trust Him by retreating, the outcomes and rewards can be amazing. What we initially perceive as failure can actually turn out to be character-enhancing opportunities. In my case, had I not obeyed God by retreating, I wouldn't have started to write about my spiritual canoe journey—my journey of faith in Jesus Chris and my journey of trusting God. I wouldn't have had the privilege of travelling across Canada as a corporate trainer. I wouldn't have had the opportunity to travel to Sub-Saharan Africa almost a dozen times as a volunteer and then senior administrator of a faith-based medical mission.

GROUP DISCUSSION
Share with the group a time when you knew you needed to retreat. What was the outcome? What new opportunities were presented? What were the rewards?

HOW DO YOU TRUST? RETREAT

9

Naomi and Ruth

In the days when the judges ruled, there was a famine in the land, and a man from Bethlehem in Judah, together with his wife and two sons, went to live for a while in the country of Moab. The man's name was Elimelech, his wife's name Naomi, and the names of his two sons were Mahlon and Kilion. They were Ephrathites from Bethlehem, Judah. And they went to Moab and lived there.

Now Elimelech, Naomi's husband, died, and she was left with her two sons. They married Moabite women, one named Orpah and the other Ruth. After they had lived there about ten years, both Mahlon and Kilion also died, and Naomi was left without her two sons and her husband.

When she heard in Moab that the Lord had come to the aid of his people by providing food for them, Naomi and her daughters-in-law prepared to return home from there. With her two daughters-in-law she left the place where she had been living and set out on the road that would take them back to the land of Judah.

Then Naomi said to her two daughters-in-law, "Go back, each of you, to your mother's home. May the Lord show kindness to you, as you have shown to your dead and to me. May the Lord grant that each of you will find rest in the home of another husband."

Then she kissed them and they wept aloud and said to her, "We will go back with you to your people."

But Naomi said, "Return home, my daughters. Why would you come with me? Am I going to have any more sons, who could become your husbands? Return home, my daughters; I am too old to have another husband. Even if I thought there was still hope for me—even if I had a husband tonight and then gave birth to sons—would you wait until they grew up? Would you remain unmarried for them? No, my daughters. It is more bitter for me than for you, because the Lord's hand has gone out against me!"

At this they wept again. Then Orpah kissed her mother-in-law good-by, but Ruth clung to her.

"Look," said Naomi, "your sister-in-law is going back to her people and her gods. Go back with her."

But Ruth replied, "Don't urge me to leave you or to turn back from you. Where you go I will go, and where you stay I will stay. Your people will be my people and your God my God. Where you die I will die, and there I will be buried. May the Lord deal with me, be it ever so severely, if anything but death separates you and me." When Naomi realized that Ruth was determined to go with her, she stopped urging her.

So the two women went on until they came to Bethlehem. When they arrived in Bethlehem, the whole town was stirred because of them, and the women exclaimed, "Can this be Naomi?"

"Don't call me Naomi," she told them. "Call me Mara, because the Almighty has made my life very bitter. I went away full, but the Lord has brought me back empty. Why call me Naomi? The Lord has afflicted me; the Almighty has brought misfortune upon me."

So Naomi returned from Moab accompanied by Ruth the Moabitess, her daughter-in-law, arriving in Bethlehem as the barley harvest was beginning.

Ruth Meets Boaz

Now Naomi had a relative on her husband's side, from the clan of Elimelech, a man of standing, whose name was Boaz.

And Ruth the Moabitess said to Naomi, "Let me go to the fields and pick up the leftover grain behind anyone in whose eyes I find favor."

Naomi said to her, "Go ahead, my daughter." So she went out and began to glean in the fields behind the harvesters. As it turned out, she found herself working in a field belonging to Boaz, who was from the clan of Elimelech.

Just then Boaz arrived from Bethlehem and greeted the harvesters, "The Lord be with you!"

"The Lord bless you!" they called back.

Boaz asked the foreman of his harvesters, "Whose young woman is that?"

The foreman replied, "She is the Moabitess who came back from Moab with Naomi. She said, 'Please let me glean and gather among the sheaves behind the harvesters.' She went into the field and has worked steadily from morning till now, except for a short rest in the shelter."

So Boaz said to Ruth, "My daughter, listen to me. Don't go and glean in another field and don't go away from here. Stay here with my servant girls. Watch the field where the men are harvesting, and follow along after the girls. I have told the men not to touch you. And whenever you are thirsty, go and get a drink from the water jars the men have filled."

At this, she bowed down with her face to the ground. She exclaimed, "Why have I found such favor in your eyes that you notice me—a foreigner?"

Boaz replied, "I've been told all about what you have done for your mother-in-law since the death of your husband—how you left your father and mother and your homeland and came to live with a people you did not know before. May the Lord repay you for what you have done. May you be richly rewarded by the Lord, the God of Israel, under whose wings you have come to take refuge."

"May I continue to find favor in your eyes, my lord," she said. *"You have given me comfort and have spoken kindly to your servant—though I do not have the standing of one of your servant girls."*

At mealtime Boaz said to her, "Come over here. Have some bread and dip it in the wine vinegar."

When she sat down with the harvesters, he offered her some roasted grain. She ate all she wanted and had some left over. As she got up to glean, Boaz gave orders to his men, "Even if she gathers among the sheaves, don't embarrass her. Rather, pull out some stalks for her from the bundles and leave them for her to pick up, and don't rebuke her."

So Ruth gleaned in the field until evening. Then she threshed the barley she had gathered, and it amounted to about an ephah. She carried it back to town, and her mother-in-law saw how much she had gathered. Ruth also brought out and gave her what she had left over after she had eaten enough.

Her mother-in-law asked her, "Where did you glean today? Where did you work? Blessed be the man who took notice of you!"

Then Ruth told her mother-in-law about the one at whose place she had been working. "The name of the man I worked with today is Boaz," she said.

"The Lord bless him!" Naomi said to her daughter-in-law. "He has not stopped showing his kindness to the living and the dead." She added, "That man is our close relative; he is one of our kinsman-redeemers."

Then Ruth the Moabitess said, "He even said to me, 'Stay with my workers until they finish harvesting all my grain.'"

Naomi said to Ruth her daughter-in-law, "It will be good for you, my daughter, to go with his girls, because in someone else's field you might be harmed."

So Ruth stayed close to the servant girls of Boaz to glean until the barley and wheat harvests were finished. And she lived with her mother-in-law. (Ruth 1:1–2:23)

Ruth was the daughter-in-law of Naomi. Naomi and her husband and two sons, all of whom were Hebrew, had left Bethlehem during a time of famine and gone to live in the country of Moab. Ruth was a Moabite who had married one of Naomi's sons. Another Moabite woman, Orpah, had married Naomi's other son. Before either of these women was able to conceive children, both of their husbands died. Naomi's husband also died, leaving her a widow. With both her sons gone, Naomi had no family in Moab to care for her. In great humility, she knew she would need to return to Bethlehem. When Naomi advised her daughters-in-law of her decision, Orpah elected to stay with her family in Moab. Ruth, however, agreed to accompany Naomi back to Bethlehem. When Naomi argued with Ruth, reminding her that she wouldn't have any other sons to whom Ruth could be given in marriage, Ruth still insisted on accompanying her.

To understand Naomi's position, we need to understand the Jewish custom of the time. If a son died prior to his wife having children, his widow would marry a brother in order to bare children. The firstborn from this second union of man and wife would be deemed the heir of the brother who had died. Thus, the family legacy would continue. In the case of Naomi and Ruth, there were no other sons. That meant Ruth was no longer obligated to be a member of Naomi's family. She was free to return to her own Moabite family and begin a new life. Ruth did choose a new life, but not the one Naomi suggested. Ruth chose a new live in Bethlehem.

Ruth was a gentile woman (in other words, a woman of stature, position, and privilege) who came from a country that worshipped heathen gods. The Moabites were known for sacrificing their children in the fire to the god of Molech. She wasn't Hebrew. Thus, when she accompanied Naomi to Bethlehem, she knew she would be an outsider, a foreigner in Israel. She would no longer be among her own people. Instead she would become like a slave in a farmer's field, trying to glean enough food for her and Naomi to eat. She would become like a servant to Naomi, ensuring her mother-in-law was well cared for. She would become a woman of no position, with seemingly no hope of a better future.

But Ruth trusted God by not paddling, by retreating with Naomi to Bethlehem. As a result of her retreat and the way she honoured Naomi, God rewarded and blessed her. Not only did she obtain favour when she gleaned in the fields (picked up the leftover wheat), she also caught the eye of Boaz, the land owner.

By reading further, we learn that she eventually became Boaz's wife. Boaz became her kinsmen redeemer by taking the place of a son Naomi no longer had. By doing so, Boaz restored honour to both Ruth and Naomi. When Ruth became pregnant and bore him a son named Obed, this son also became known as Naomi's grandson. According to Hebrew law, he would therefore ensure the lineage of Mahlon (Ruth's first husband and Naomi's dead son). Obed became the father of Jesse, and Jesse became the father of David. As we read further in the Bible, we learn that Jesus Christ was a descendent of David, meaning that Ruth played an important role in the lineage of Jesus Christ.

If we were to reflect upon Ruth's character, we would conclude that she was a woman of consistency. She was not one to waiver. Upon careful consideration, she would make wise choices. She was humble, industrious, and obedient, and despite her gentile upbringing she was a true handmaiden. She honoured her mother-in-law and accepted counsel from her. She was a foreigner, a servant who was exalted into a royal line.

Because Ruth wasn't inflexible, insensitive, stubborn, prideful, or envious, her retreat posture was rewarded. Not only did she become the wife of Boaz, an esteemed man of great wealth, she became one of the few women identified in the lineage of Jesus.

I would like to dwell for a moment on the decision Naomi made—one of retreat. Knowing that Naomi was retreating to Bethlehem totally humiliated, Ruth was willing to join her. By the simple matter of association, Ruth would be in a position of humiliation as well, probably even more so because she was a Moabite. Ruth trusted God… the God she knew only through Naomi's witness and example.

MY STORY

One of the meanings of retreat is a movement away from danger or confrontation, or a movement back along one's original route.

Did I need to move away from danger? No. However, I did need to move back from a position of confrontation. The phrase "hell has no fury as a woman scorned" comes to mind. I had been scorned, rejected, and abandoned. My husband was choosing a future without me in it. He was making decisions to sell our home, to purchase his new residence, and split all our furnishings. He had asked me to get a lawyer, open up my own bank account, and arrange for my own credit cards. He had told me to start moving on without him.

Did I choose to confront? Initially, yes, I did. It was more from a posture of begging that Jim chose not to sell our home right away but instead enter into a rental arrangement. In his mind, this was so I could get used to the idea of having a life and home without him around.

The best illustration for moving away or backing down from a position is "my list." Yes, I had given God a list. I had accepted the fact that God was in control, that in His infinite wisdom this was a season in our lives for which we needed to be apart. I was starting to believe Jim would eventually come back. However, there was no way I was going to let him back into my life and into our home without some noticeable changes. I had actually said to God that I would take him back only if and when… and then came the long list. I regularly said, "God, you will need to change him." After what he had put me through, there was no way Jim was ever going to calmly walk back into our lives unchanged, as if nothing had happened.

God then asked me to read the book of Hosea. Hmm! Here was a man God had instructed to marry an unredeemed prostitute. When she ran away, did he bid her good riddance? No. Instead, he ran after her and brought her home. Even though she was unchanged, Hosea loved her. He abandoned his position and chose God's position of grace, mercy, and forgiveness.

As a result, I had to abandon my position. No list. Only forgiveness! When Jim came back (and I believed it was a matter of "when," not "if"), he could come home unchanged. I had to move away from my own self-righteousness and offer him forgiveness, love, grace, mercy, kindness, and goodness every time he came around.

95

Consider how Ruth acted when she retreated with Naomi to Bethlehem. Ruth didn't hide in Naomi's home. Ruth was an industrious handmaiden who went out and worked. She didn't sit idly by and sulk at her window, pining for days gone by. Ruth became very active. So much so that I suspect she came home every evening absolutely exhausted after gleaning in the fields.

Ah. So *that* was what I needed to do as I took this posture of retreat. I needed to remain active and engaged. I needed to work. I needed to volunteer. I needed to spend time with family. I needed to enjoy my grandchildren by spending more time baking cookies and playing board games. I needed to spend more time enjoying my two sons, watching one excel as a hockey player and encouraging the other as he provided for his young family. I needed to spend more time with my mom, travelling to visit her and getting to know her better. I needed to spend more time with friends and focus on encouraging them. I knew that as I prayed for them and served their needs, God would take care of my needs and I would have less time to focus on what I thought I had lost.

In this season of trusting God through retreat, I was not to be idle. I was to be industrious and not let my lamp go out at night. I was to allow God to weave the attributes of the Proverbs 31 woman into my life (see Proverbs 31).

Scriptures for Reflection

Where you go I will go, and where you stay I will stay. Your people will be my people and your God my God. (Ruth 1:16)

_____

_____

_____

_____

_____

_____

Let me go to the fields… (Ruth 2:2)

_____

_____

_____

_____

_____

_____

Please let me glean and gather among the sheaves behind the harvesters. (Ruth 2:6)

_____

_____

_____

_____

_____

_____

PERSONAL LEADERSHIP EXAMPLE

After being involved as the director of Canadian operations for a faith-based medical mission for eight years, God told me to step away because He had something better. In this situation, I was not to remain passive. God could choose to miraculously provide for this ministry. Instead God told me to retreat.

Some said I was jumping ship. Others said I was running away from the inevitable. I wasn't persevering and running the race of the champion, going for the prize. I wasn't being patient. I wasn't letting go and letting God.

God told me to leave. He didn't tell me to go forward into another job. He didn't tell me to start something new. He told me to retreat—to rest awhile, to move into a place of rest, of refuge, of reclusiveness so He could speak with me, encourage me, and rejuvenate me.

In other words, God was asking me to trust Him by retreating because He wanted to sew a seed that would begin a new season in my life. Or possibly He wanted to reveal something in my character that He wanted to address privately.

God asked me to leave a position and organization I had thought I would enjoy for the rest of my career. I began to question if I would ever be in a place for any length of time. I began to doubt the marketability of my resume. An executive search professional would have deemed me unstable by not staying in any one organization for any length of time. In the natural, why was I always resigning? If I was going to fear the opinions and conclusions of man, this would be the time. Instead I had to rely on my trust in God. I had to trust God to know that He ultimately had my best interests at heart. God had another place for me, another role for me to play. He had other situations for me to encounter and a new group of people to influence.

I had to trust God when He said, "What you're doing is good. However, what I have planned for you is better." What did "better" look like? I had no idea. Was I going into the "better" place right away? No. First I had to retreat. Retreat doesn't mean failure. Retreat can actually be the safest place in the world—especially if you know God has asked you to trust Him by going there.

GROUP DISCUSSION

When you chose a posture of retreat, did you have family and friends who didn't understand and began to question or accuse you of not being in God's will? Share with the group how you handled the situation.

Hezekiah: Known as a King

> *Hezekiah trusted in the Lord, the God of Israel. There was no one like him among all the kings of Judah, either before him or after him.* (2 Kings 18:5)

Sennacherib Threatens Jerusalem

> *After all that Hezekiah had so faithfully done, Sennacherib king of Assyria came and invaded Judah. He laid siege to the fortified cities, thinking to conquer them for himself. When Hezekiah saw that Sennacherib had come and that he intended to make war on Jerusalem, he consulted with his officials and military staff about blocking off the water from the springs outside the city, and they helped him. A large force of men assembled, and they blocked all the springs and the stream that flowed through the land. "Why should the kings of Assyria come and find plenty of water?" they said. Then he worked hard repairing all the broken sections of the wall and building towers on it. He built another wall outside that one and reinforced the supporting terraces of the City of David. He also made large numbers of weapons and shields.*

He appointed military officers over the people and assembled them before him in the square at the city gate and encouraged them with these words: "Be strong and courageous. Do not be afraid or discouraged because of the king of Assyria and the vast army with him, for there is a greater power with us than with him. With him is only the arm of flesh, but with us is the Lord our God to help us and to fight our battles." And the people gained confidence from what Hezekiah the king of Judah said.

Later, when Sennacherib king of Assyria and all his forces were laying siege to Lachish, he sent his officers to Jerusalem with this message for Hezekiah king of Judah and for all the people of Judah who were there:

"This is what Sennacherib king of Assyria says: On what are you basing your confidence, that you remain in Jerusalem under siege? When Hezekiah says, 'The Lord our God will save us from the hand of the king of Assyria,' he is misleading you, to let you die of hunger and thirst. Did not Hezekiah himself remove this god's high places and altars, saying to Judah and Jerusalem, 'You must worship before one altar and burn sacrifices on it'?

"Do you not know what I and my fathers have done to all the peoples of the other lands? Were the gods of those nations ever able to deliver their land from my hand? Who of all the gods of these nations that my fathers destroyed has been able to save his people from me? How then can your god deliver you from my hand? Now do not let Hezekiah deceive you and mislead you like this. Do not believe him, for no god of any nation or kingdom has been able to deliver his people from my hand or the hand of my fathers. How much less will your god deliver you from my hand!"

Sennacherib's officers spoke further against the Lord God and against his servant Hezekiah. The king also wrote letters insulting the Lord, the God of Israel, and saying this against him: "Just as the gods of the peoples of the other lands did not rescue their people from my hand, so the god of Hezekiah will not rescue his people from my hand." Then they called out in Hebrew to the people of Jerusalem who were on the wall, to terrify them and make them afraid in order to capture the city. They spoke about the God of Jerusalem as they did about the gods of the other peoples of the world—the work of men's hands.

King Hezekiah and the prophet Isaiah son of Amoz cried out in prayer to heaven about this. And the Lord sent an angel, who annihilated all the fighting men and the leaders and officers in the camp of the Assyrian king. So he withdrew to his own land in disgrace. And when he went into the temple of his god, some of his sons cut him down with the sword.

So the Lord saved Hezekiah and the people of Jerusalem from the hand of Sennacherib king of Assyria and from the hand of all others. He took care of them on every side. Many brought offerings to Jerusalem for the Lord and valuable gifts for Hezekiah king of Judah. From then on he was highly regarded by all the nations. (2 Chronicles 32:1–23)

I love the story of Hezekiah. Although many stories in the Old Testament illustrate man's ability to trust God, I find Hezekiah's situation to be the most compelling. We don't need to assume or even infer that he trusted God. The scripture actually says that he trusted God, that there was no one like him among all the kings of Judah before or after—not even King David.

Imagine being in a position of favour with God. We know this because the passage states that Hezekiah had been faithful. Those who are faithful receive favour because God rewards those who are faithful. However, in this situation, it doesn't appear Hezekiah was receiving favour. Sennacherib, a mighty foreign king, sought to conquer Jerusalem. What did Hezekiah do when he learned that this king intended to make war? Did he become passive? He could have said that because of his trust, God would intervene. God had intervened powerfully with his ancestors, so He could do so again now. King Hezekiah also could have retreated. Learning of all the death and destruction, Hezekiah could have taken all the citizens of Jerusalem and fled to Egypt for sanctuary. Instead he chose to stay and take a stand.

By taking a stand, did Hezekiah simply send letters articulating his ultimate authority to the foreign king and wave the enemy off as not being a viable threat? Did he think to do his own part to ensure his enemy's defeat, just in case God wasn't able? No. King Hezekiah took up a posture of assertiveness, because he knew he had to become actively engaged. Even though he trusted God, he needed to do his part. Yes, he knew God could slay the enemy even before they reached Jerusalem, but what if God had a different plan? Hezekiah wasn't God and didn't know God's purpose for this invasion.

Sometimes when we see people "doing their part," we conclude that they don't trust God, that they don't believe God can give them the victory. In our minds, we think, "What if God doesn't show up? If it were me, I would be prepared, just in case." That's certainly not a posture of trust. That type of thinking demonstrates unbelief.

Hezekiah didn't do just one token thing to "do his part." He did many things. He was strategic and tactical. Through seeking counsel with the prophet, a strategy was developed. Through seeking engagement with his military officials, a tactical offence and defence was planned.

He consulted with his officials and military staff about blocking off water from the springs outside the city. Hezekiah didn't tell them to help. Because he asked for their advice and opinion, a large force of men assembled and blocked all the springs. By not letting the enemy find water, he denied them the ability to live.

He worked hard to repair all the broken sections of the wall, and built towers on them. He built a second wall outside the first and reinforced the supporting terraces. He also made large numbers of weapons and shields.

He appointed military officers over the people and assembled them before him in the square at the city gate. He encouraged them. He declared that there was a greater power with them than was with the enemy. The enemy was only flesh and bones, but with them was the Lord our God, who would help fight their battles. Hezekiah didn't say God would actually fight their battles. He said that God would *help* them fight their battles.

To put this illustration into a modern-day perspective, God has given us eight simple steps to overthrow our enemies. We don't just rely on God. Instead we rely on our partnership with the Lord, whereby we exercise our own faith and beliefs.

Step 1. Consult with those closest to you for advice (your pastor, your prayer partners, your Bible study group).

Step 2. Block off the water so the enemy has no way of getting to you. Determine any activities you are involved with, programs you watch or books you read or friendships you encourage that are influencing you away from God.

Step 3. Repair the broken sections of your life. Determine where there are broken relationships due to unforgiveness, bitterness, envy, or jealousy. Seek these individuals and ask forgiveness and mercy.

Step 4. Build towers around your life. Ensure the people around you will watch out for you, step in and protect you, and pray and intercede for you.

Step 5. Place a secondary wall around your life by building up your faith, the faith that comes from reading God's word.

Step 6. Make weapons and shields (for spiritual warfare). Ensure that you know how to put on the armour God has given you and that you know how to use all the weapons at your disposal (the helmet of salvation, sword of the spirit, breastplate of righteousness, shield of faith, belt of truth, and feed shod in preparation with the gospel and prayer).

Step 7. Appoint military officers. In other words, surround yourself with people of encouragement who will build you up and remind you to be strong and courageous.

Step 8. Cry out to God in prayer so He will send His angels to protect you.

MY STORY

Shortly after Jim left, I sought God to learn if there was anything I was doing (or not doing) that had contributed to the demise of our relationship. What might I have been responsible for that would have caused my husband to decide he didn't want to be married to me anymore? I looked at the set of instructions God gave Hezekiah and began to invoke them in my own life.

I had called my pastor and two best friends, asking them to join me in prayer. They provided me with wise counsel.

I asked God to show me areas of my life where I may have been giving the enemy a foothold. I asked God to help me close off the entry to the springs so the enemy would no longer be fed.

I asked God to show me if there was any unforgiveness in my life. Was I envious or jealous? Did I need to repent for any wrongdoings or acts of unrighteousness before my friends and family?

I ensured that I continued to be in relationship with other believers so we could pray together. I wanted to ensure I had those around me who would lift me up when I was too weak to carry on.

I increased the amount of time I spent reading God's word and ensured that I put on the full spiritual armour of God every day. I wanted to be prepared for all the lies of the enemy.

I maintained my relationships with family, friends, co-workers, and those in places of leadership so they could support me when I was too weak to stand. Rather than withdrawing from those around me, I pursued their friendships.

Finally, I prayed… and prayed… and prayed…

Scriptures for Reflection

Hezekiah trusted in the Lord, the God of Israel. There was no we like him among all the kings of Judah, either before him or after him. (2 Kings 18:5)

_____
_____
_____
_____
_____
_____

With him is only the arm of flesh, but with us is the Lord our God to help us and to fight our battles. (2 Chronicles 32:8)

_____
_____
_____
_____
_____
_____

King Hezekiah and the prophet Isaiah son of Amoz cried out in prayer to heaven about this. (2 Chronicles 32:20)

_____
_____
_____
_____
_____
_____

PERSONAL LEADERSHIP EXAMPLE

At one point in my career, I needed to lead a ministry through a season of trusting God in a posture of assertiveness. After calling one of our bimonthly prayer meetings, I read to the group the passage from 2 Chronicles. I reminded everyone that our founder's initial trust in God had birthed this ministry. Because of the foundation of faith laid at the beginning of this medical work in East Africa, we knew God would continue to be with us.

We were surrounded by the enemies of doubt, stress, weariness, unclear direction, and diverging leadership styles. The founder and his family had been in Africa for about ten years, and the organization that had formed around him had been in place for seven years. The leadership in the country had changed and all the founding board members had moved on. Although we still operated as a faith-based medical organization and all those in leadership were believers in the Lordship of Jesus Christ, God had allowed us to be placed in a situation whereby we had to exercise Hezekiah's strategies in order to be victorious.

Step 1. We needed to continue to meet as a joint leadership team and not be divided due to geographical limitations. We needed to continue our board and committee meetings. We obtained counsel during leadership meetings and staff planning sessions

Step 2. Had we gotten involved in activities that weren't sanctioned by God? Had we accepted funding from individuals or organizations that were trying to influence us away from our initial vision? At that time, we received funding from the Global Fund, European tobacco foundations, American medical organizations, other Christian ministries, and many philanthropic individuals. We accepted volunteers from all walks of faith as long as they acknowledged that we were Christians. Although those in leadership possessed the core values of belief in Jesus Christ, our paid staff, volunteers, and benefactors didn't need to have the same core values.

Step 3. We needed to review our lists of donors. Had we offended any of them? Had we not thanked them for their generous gifts? Did any of our suppliers refuse to deal with us anymore? Were we up to date with all our bill payments? Were we honouring the local government through the payment of all applicable taxes? Were our mission teams being truthful when they brought medical supplies and gifts through customs? Were we beyond reproach, operating with integrity?

Step 4. Did we have enough groups and individuals praying for the success of our ministry? Sure, we met regularly for corporate prayer, but were those who funded us also praying for us? We needed to contact our supporting churches and let them know how they could best pray for us. We needed to contact all our donors to apprise them of our situation, so that they, in turn, could pray for us.

Step 5. Were we operating with a measure of faith similar to that which was exercised by our founding doctor when he first went to the mission field? Not really. We were all trying to do this on our own strength.

Step 6. Did everyone involved in the ministry know how to use their spiritual weapons? Did everyone have on their helmet of salvation? Were they operating with righteousness and truth? Was there any deception amongst us that needed to be weeded out?

Step 7. Did we have the right people in the right places of leadership? Was everyone being exhorted to be strong and courageous and not to fear? Although the enemy appeared to be powerful, did we know and understand that God was with us and thus we were more powerful?

Step 8. Finally, how were our corporate and individual prayer lives?

GROUP DISCUSSION

Describe a situation in your life when God helped you to fight your battle. When did you paddle your canoe because God told you to pick up the paddles? Were there times when God didn't remove the enemy, but instead prepared you and appeared to fight (paddle) alongside you?

Abigail: Known as a Conciliator

David, Nabal and Abigail

Now Samuel died, and all Israel assembled and mourned for
him; and they buried him at his home in Ramah. Then David
moved down into the Desert of Maon.

A certain man in Maon, who had property there at Carmel,
was very wealthy. He had a thousand goats and three thousand
sheep, which he was shearing in Carmel. His name was Nabal and
his wife's name was Abigail. She was an intelligent and beautiful
woman, but her husband, a Calebite, was surly and mean in his
dealings.

While David was in the desert, he heard that Nabal was
shearing sheep. So he sent ten young men and said to them, "Go up
to Nabal at Carmel and greet him in my name. Say to him: 'Long
life to you! Good health to you and your household! And good health
to all that is yours!

"'Now I hear that it is sheep-shearing time. When your
shepherds were with us, we did not mistreat them, and the whole
time they were at Carmel nothing of theirs was missing. Ask your
own servants and they will tell you. Therefore be favorable toward

my young men, since we come at a festive time. Please give your servants and your son David whatever you can find for them.'"

When David's men arrived, they gave Nabal this message in David's name. Then they waited.

Nabal answered David's servants, "Who is this David? Who is this son of Jesse? Many servants are breaking away from their masters these days. Why should I take my bread and water, and the meat I have slaughtered for my shearers, and give it to men coming from who knows where?"

David's men turned around and went back. When they arrived, they reported every word. David said to his men, "Put on your swords!" So they put on their swords, and David put on his. About four hundred men went up with David, while two hundred stayed with the supplies.

One of the servants told Nabal's wife Abigail: "David sent messengers from the desert to give our master his greetings, but he hurled insults at them. Yet these men were very good to us. They did not mistreat us, and the whole time we were out in the fields near them nothing was missing. Night and day they were a wall around us all the time we were herding our sheep near them. Now think it over and see what you can do, because disaster is hanging over our master and his whole household. He is such a wicked man that no one can talk to him."

Abigail lost no time. She took two hundred loaves of bread, two skins of wine, five dressed sheep, five seahs of roasted grain, a hundred cakes of raisins and two hundred cakes of pressed figs, and loaded them on donkeys. Then she told her servants, "Go on ahead; I'll follow you." But she did not tell her husband Nabal.

As she came riding her donkey into a mountain ravine, there were David and his men descending toward her, and she met them. David had just said, "It's been useless—all my watching over this fellow's property in the desert so that nothing of his was missing. He has paid me back evil for good. May God deal with David, be it ever so severely, if by morning I leave alive one male of all who belong to him!"

When Abigail saw David, she quickly got off her donkey and bowed down before David with her face to the ground. She fell at his feet and said: "My lord, let the blame be on me alone. Please let your servant speak to you; hear what your servant has to say. May my lord pay no attention to that wicked man Nabal. He is just like his name—his name is Fool, and folly goes with him. But as for me, your servant, I did not see the men my master sent.

"Now since the Lord has kept you, my master, from bloodshed and from avenging yourself with your own hands, as surely as the Lord lives and as you live, may your enemies and all who intend to harm my master be like Nabal. And let this gift, which your servant has brought to my master, be given to the men who follow you.

Please forgive your servant's offense, for the Lord will certainly make a lasting dynasty for my master, because he fights the Lord's battles. Let no wrongdoing be found in you as long as you live. Even though someone is pursuing you to take your life, the life of my master will be bound securely in the bundle of the living by the Lord your God. But the lives of your enemies he will hurl away as from the pocket of a sling. When the Lord has done for my master every good thing he promised concerning him and has appointed him leader over Israel, my master will not have on his conscience the staggering burden of needless bloodshed or of having avenged himself. And when the Lord has brought my master success, remember your servant."

David said to Abigail, "Praise be to the Lord, the God of Israel, who has sent you today to meet me. May you be blessed for your good judgment and for keeping me from bloodshed this day and from avenging myself with my own hands. Otherwise, as surely as the Lord, the God of Israel, lives, who has kept me from harming you, if you had not come quickly to meet me, not one male belonging to Nabal would have been left alive by daybreak."

Then David accepted from her hand what she had brought him and said, "Go home in peace. I have heard your words and granted your request."

When Abigail went to Nabal, he was in the house holding a banquet like that of a king. He was in high spirits and very drunk.

So she told him nothing until daybreak. Then in the morning, when Nabal was sober, his wife told him all these things, and his heart failed him and he became like a stone. About ten days later, the Lord struck Nabal and he died.

When David heard that Nabal was dead, he said, "Praise be to the Lord, who has upheld my cause against Nabal for treating me with contempt. He has kept his servant from doing wrong and has brought Nabal's wrongdoing down on his own head."

Then David sent word to Abigail, asking her to become his wife. His servants went to Carmel and said to Abigail, "David has sent us to you to take you to become his wife."

She bowed down with her face to the ground and said, "Here is your maidservant, ready to serve you and wash the feet of my master's servants." Abigail quickly got on a donkey and, attended by her five maids, went with David's messengers and became his wife. David had also married Ahinoam of Jezreel, and they both were his wives. But Saul had given his daughter Michal, David's wife, to Paltiel son of Laish, who was from Gallim. (1Samuel: 25: 1 - 41)

This story takes place during a time when David and Saul (the first king of Israel) were at war. The prophet Samuel, who had anointed Saul as king, had died. David and his men had moved down into the desert of Paran. Many of the servants of Nabel, a prominent landowner, had joined with David in support of his efforts against King Saul. At sheep-shearing time, however, many of these men had to return to their master, Nabel, in order to assist him. While David was in the area, close to Nabel's land holdings, he sent ten men to ask Nabel to provide them with provisions. Nabel refused to grant David's request. However, one of Nabel's servants told Nabel's wife Abigail of Nabel's refusal. The servant told Abigail that he was afraid Nabel's household would suffer retribution.

When Abigail heard about David's request from one of Nabel's servants, who had also served in David's army, she lost no time in feeding David's troops. She heeded this servant's warning despite knowing she was disobeying her husband.

When we read this story, we learn that Abigail trusted God more than she feared man. Although she knew Saul was her king, she knew David fought the Lord's battles. She knew King Saul was pursuing David and that he had hidden with his army on their land. She also knew that because he had been on their land, he had protected their household. His army had protected them from King Saul and his army, not to mention the unruly men within David's camp. David was quite within his rights to ask Nabel for provisions. It would be no different than those who serve in our armed forces and protect our land to expect to be paid and receive food and shelter. Nabel, whose name means "fool," was too pompous and arrogant to even acknowledge that his wealth and status had much to do with the protection David provided.

Whether David would have actually brought bloodshed upon Nabel's family isn't up for discussion. Here, we're addressing Abigail's willful disobedience by refusing to obey her husband and instead honouring the request of a stranger. It's also interesting that although David may have originally sought vengeance, it was God who acted upon it and struck Nabel dead. Nabel had not honoured God's anointed.

As a result of Abigail's faith and assertive demonstration of trust, she and the remaining members of her household were saved. When David learned of Nabel's death, he became Abigail's redeemer. Rather than seeing her become a potentially forgotten and forsaken widow, David asked her to become his third wife.

When I look at the posture of assertive trust in another light, I think of other characteristics that are inherent to this posture. Abigail was intelligent. She was beautiful. She operated as a servant and conciliator. She possessed good judgment and wasn't afraid of the consequences of her decision. She was a capable and dignified woman.

Abigail was not dishonourable. She chose to honour God above her husband—a difficult choice to make. She wasn't a manipulator or accomplice to murder. In other words, her actions didn't result in her husband's death. It was the hand of God that struck Nabel dead, as punishment for his actions. Abigail trusted God. She took care of God's needs by feeding David's army, and God took care of her needs by providing justice for her situation. Abigail wasn't a covetous woman.

She didn't aspire to be a member of David's court, let alone his wife. Her motive was simply to operate as God had directed her.

In this instance, we can see that there are rewards given when we trust God. What reward did Abigail receive? She received the love of King David, a worshipper and man after God's own heart. She received position. Even though, as a widow, she would have lost all her privileges, God rewarded her with a higher position. Instead of being the wife of a wealthy landowner, she became the wife of a king.

Many of us may struggle with this story, as it appears as though she dishonoured and disobeyed her husband. However, we need to understand all that transpired. David was esteemed and Abigail knew that the favour of God was upon him. Firstly, Abigail and Nabel's servants had been released from their duties on the ranch to serve in David's army. Despite the needs of David and his company, David had released these same servants to assist Nabel during sheep-shearing time. Why would Nabel not return the favour by providing for David? Was Nabel's heart cold? Was he selfish? Was he angry at David for taking his servants in the first place?

None of these reasons matter. Abigail knew her God. She knew what was right and true. She knew that she was to provide hospitality to those in her midst. She knew that obeying God was more important than obeying an ungodly command from her husband. She must have counted the cost, knowing that her husband's wrath may come upon her. However, she trusted God to protect her because she knew what she was doing was right.

We must become capable and use the resources and talents God has given us. We need to exercise good judgment in using these talents with dignity.

MY STORY: THE MEAT PIE

Christmas season was upon us and my parents announced that they were coming to visit me and my son. Although I told them that I no longer had a furnished spare bedroom where they could sleep, my mother insisted that they needed to be here. When I tried to convince her otherwise, she told me that I needed her.

Wow! That was a powerful statement. Many years prior, when I had asked my mom to come and be with me for a while, she refused. I had been suffering from a nervous breakdown and felt incapable, as a single mother, to care for my young son. Now here she was, almost twenty years later, saying that I needed her. Even though I hadn't asked (I was probably too stubborn to do so), she insisted on coming.

Preparations were made for their arrival. I placed my son on an air mattress in the spare room and I occupied the single bed in his room. My parents had the luxury of sleeping in the master bedroom, enjoying the king-size bed and full master bathroom. I announced to Jim that my parents were going to be around for about a week so that he would be forewarned when he came to pick up our son for hockey games or practices.

Each time Jim came around, my mother watched how I reacted and spoke to him. Was I operating with bitterness, hatred, and rejection? Was I cold, uncaring, and abrupt when he came to the door or called on the phone? Not at all. Thanks to God's grace, I was able to operate with love and kindness each time Jim came to our home, so much so that Mom thought it important that Jim join us on Christmas Day for turkey dinner rather than being alone.

Now, think about this for a moment. You and your husband are estranged. Your parents are in town and it's already an emotionally charged time of year. Now you also need to entertain your husband—a man who abandoned you—on Christmas Day, in front of your family. Whew! Would I be able to do this? Well, in Christ I could do all things, right? I decided to extend an invitation; Jim wouldn't need to be alone on Christmas Day.

Accepting the fact that Jim was going to be around on Christmas Day was about to become the easy part. The seed of grace and forgiveness that had been sown through my mother's words soon manifested through an act of kindness that God would personally instruct me to do.

Every year throughout our marriage, Jim and I had a tradition of enjoying a homemade meat pie on Christmas Eve. This tortierre would take the majority of the day to make and would be served to family and guests prior to attending the Christmas Eve service. Initially, I felt no need to take the time and effort to make the meat pie this year. It wasn't one of my family's traditions, nor was it expected as a meal on Christmas Eve.

The day before Christmas Eve, though, I knew I needed to make this meat pie. I was compelled to drive to the grocery store, pick up all the ingredients, and then spend the next day making it. The aroma of simmering seasoned meat brought anticipation to everyone in the home. You can imagine their dismay when I announced that we weren't eating before the five o'clock service, like usual. Instead I wrapped up the pie in towels and dropped it off at Jim's rented home on the way to church. We would eat after church once we arrived at my cousin's open house Christmas Eve family gathering.

I imagine that my parents were stunned when I drove up to Jim's house, got out of the car, and knocked on his door only to find that no one was home. Would I bring the meat pie back in the car for all of us to enjoy later? No. I left it on his doorstep, wrapped up in a box.

I learned after the fact that this simple act of kindness was the turning point in our separation. When Jim saw the meat pie and knew how much time and effort it had taken me to prepare it, and that it was only for him to enjoy, he saw God's mercy at work. Instead of getting what he deserved—the shunning of his rejected wife, he witnessed the mercy of God in a very practical way. Despite being estranged from his family, he was still going to be able to enjoy one of his favourite family traditions—a meat pie at Christmas.

Scriptures for Reflection

Abigail lost no time. (1 Samuel 25:18)

_____

_____

_____

_____

_____

_____

_____

May you be blessed for your judgment... (1 Samuel 25:33)

_____

_____

_____

_____

_____

_____

Who will rise up for me against the wicked? Who will take a stand for me against evildoers? (Psalm 94:16)

_____

_____

_____

_____

_____

_____

_____

PERSONAL LEADERSHIP EXAMPLE

There is a brief blip in my career which I don't identify on my resume. In my early years of involvement with a particular organization, a lot of my work was voluntary. When I did eventually start to be remunerated, the salary was minimal. As a result, I supplemented my income by taking a position with a timeshare company. In this role, I reported to the vice-president of finance. From a career perspective, this was a step down because I had held the vice-president of finance position in two previous organizations, with managerial staff reporting to me.

When I arrived, the environment was somewhat chaotic. Leadership was almost non-existent and the company was acquiring several new properties that needed to be integrated into the parent organization. It soon became apparent that I was expected to perform more than my expected day-to-day functions. The ever-growing accounting department was in significant need of leadership, coaching, mentoring, and encouragement. Although the vice-president of finance was competent, he wasn't known for his people skills.

Despite the lack of a corporate culture that encouraged mentorship, I took on the challenge of investing in my subordinates. I had an excellent group of individuals who were capable of excelling. They had much to bring to the organization, if encouraged. The morale of the department began to change as I implemented regular staff meetings, one-on-one mentoring sessions, and team problem-solving sessions. Those in the executive offices noted the changes, as well as the improvements being made in terms of the timeliness and accuracy of the financial reporting.

When it was decided to bring in new accounting software, the search for an appropriate program began. Although I believed their current platform was more than capable of accommodating any and all future growth they aspired to, I was asked to help analyse these new products. At this point in my career, I had been involved in several different conversions from one accounting program to another. I had installed a brand-new system in an educational facility. I had transitioned the management enterprise system in another organization away from several standalone programs. As a result, I could have been deemed an expert on evaluating programs, leading transition teams, and managing employees at a time of significant change.

However, that was not my role. I provided input and the vice-president of finance made the decision. Although I disagreed with his reasoning and the ultimate choice he made, I supported his decision and ensured that all the staff was brought alongside.

Very quickly, it became apparent that my supervisor wasn't up to the challenge. As the days and weeks progressed, I was brought into more and more decision-making meetings. With next to no support, and limited information, I led the team to the best of my ability, all the while honouring and respecting the leadership God had subjected me to.

How does this story relate to trusting God through a position of assertiveness? It sounds more like a position of submission. Well, I learned that we can actually be in a position of submission and still be assertive. Remember Abigail. She operated in a position of submission to her husband, yet when she had to stand up for her beliefs and make a decision, she chose to be assertive. In other words, she took action.

That's exactly what I was called to do at this company. Although I was more qualified than my current boss, I chose the position of submission—at least, in the natural. In the spirit, I was operating with assertiveness. I stood in the gap for my staff. No longer would I tolerate them being bullied by my boss. I ensured that they were rewarded with professional development opportunities and nonfinancial benefits, even though it wasn't within the culture of the organization to do so. I ensured that everyone within my sphere of influence was treated with respect, regardless of who they were or what their job entailed.

As a result of my skillsets and professional strengths, my peers began to see me as more deserving of the vice-president role than the incumbent. I asked God if I was to stay in this environment. I continued to trust God, constantly asking for wisdom on how to walk through this season.

Then a couple of events occurred that influenced my decision. I knew God hadn't allowed me to be employed at this organization so I could usurp my boss's authority and take over his position. I knew I was only to be there for a season. How long of a season, I didn't know. While I was doing my best to honour my boss and ensure that my staff respected him, regardless of his shortcomings, God began to open other opportunities for me.

My first book had just been published and copies were starting to sell. In addition, the organization for which I had been volunteering was now in a position to employ me for more hours each week. Although the pay continued to be below industry average, I trusted God on what He was going to do with my book.

It took an assertive and courageous act for me to tender my resignation. I had to trust God and lay down my paddles. As a result, a man's integrity was kept intact, co-workers were led to salvation through their belief in Jesus Christ, and God opened doors for me to speak at women's events around the world.

GROUP DISCUSSION

In your current position, are you known as a conciliator? Do you possess good judgment, discerning the difference between God's commands and man's selfish orders? Share an example of a time when you took a stand for righteousness. Did God ask you to paddle?

Asa: Known as a King

Asa King of Judah

Asa did what was good and right in the eyes of the Lord his God. He removed the foreign altars and the high places, smashed the sacred stones and cut down the Asherah poles. He commanded Judah to seek the Lord, the God of their fathers, and to obey his laws and commands. He removed the high places and incense altars in every town in Judah, and the kingdom was at peace under him. He built up the fortified cities of Judah, since the land was at peace. No one was at war with him during those years, for the Lord gave him rest.

"Let us build up these towns," he said to Judah, "and put walls around them, with towers, gates and bars. The land is still ours, because we have sought the Lord our God; we sought him and he has given us rest on every side." So they built and prospered.

Asa had an army of three hundred thousand men from Judah, equipped with large shields and with spears, and two hundred and eighty thousand from Benjamin, armed with small shields and with bows. All these were brave fighting men.

Zerah the Cushite marched out against them with a vast army and three hundred chariots, and came as far as Mareshah. Asa went out to meet him, and they took up battle positions in the Valley of Zephathah near Mareshah. Then Asa called to the Lord his God and said, "Lord, there is no one like you to help the powerless against the mighty. Help us, O Lord our God, for we rely on you, and in your name we have come against this vast army. O Lord, you are our God; do not let man prevail against you."

The Lord struck down the Cushites before Asa and Judah. The Cushites fled, and Asa and his army pursued them as far as Gerar. Such a great number of Cushites fell that they could not recover; they were crushed before the Lord and his forces. The men of Judah carried off a large amount of plunder. They destroyed all the villages around Gerar, for the terror of the Lord had fallen upon them. They plundered all these villages, since there was much booty there. They also attacked the camps of the herdsmen and carried off droves of sheep and goats and camels. Then they returned to Jerusalem. (2 Chronicles 14:2–15)

Asa's reign as king of Israel occurred several generations after King David, and several generations before King Hezekiah. The original twelve tribes of Israel were now divided into two kingdoms—Israel and Judah. The ten northern tribes were known as Israel and the remaining two tribes (Judah and Benjamin) were known as Judah. King David was Asa's great-great-grandfather.

As we can read from the story, King Asa did what was good and right in the eyes of the Lord. He obeyed God and encouraged all within his kingdom to obey God's laws and commandments. He knew the protection they would receive from God because they were obedient. He trusted God's word.

Despite his belief and trust in God and His word, he didn't remain in a position of passivity or complacency. Even though the land was at peace and the Lord had given him rest, he continued to build up the fortified cities of Judah. He put walls around these cities, constructed towers, and placed gates and bars in them. He knew that because they had sought the Lord, God had given them rest from all their adversaries. King Asa didn't stop with these symbols of strength, though. He also equipped thousands of men with shields, spears, and bows—both in the territory of Judah as well as the territory of Benjamin. These were brave fighting men.

Considering King Asa found favour with God, wouldn't you think God would protect him on all occasions? Why would he have to dwell in fortified cities? If King Asa trusted God, why was he compelled to have large armies around him? Actually, it was *because* he trusted God that he built those cities and equipped his men for battle. He knew God was preparing them for a time when they would need to trust Him during battle, a time when they wouldn't be able to rely on their own strength, despite how vast it appeared.

That time came when Zerah the Cushite marched against King Asa. Although Zerah had a vast army of three hundred thousand chariots, King Asa went out to meet him, without any chariots and accompanied by men equipped with shields, spears, and bows. Asa didn't wait in one of the fortified cities for the enemy to come. He didn't retreat or run from the enemy because he knew the enemy was stronger. No, Asa trusted God and went out, away from all his symbols of safety and protection, to engage the enemy in battle at Mareshah.

What happened next is powerful. Asa had trusted God by taking that first step. However, he never had to raise his weapons against the enemy or step any further than where God had called him. Asa knew the enemy wasn't fighting against them as men, but against their God. He prayed and stated that there was no one like the Lord to help the powerless against the mighty. He knew God would help them because they relied on Him. He knew it was in God's name that the enemy had come against them with this vast army. He knew God wouldn't allow men to prevail against God.

Another miraculous victory occurred. Without King Asa or any member of his army lifting a weapon, God intervened. The Lord struck down the enemy and they fled to the land of Cush. King Asa and his army pursued them, taking back all that the enemy had plundered.

MY STORY

During the time of our separation, there were a few occasions when my posture of trusting God took on an aggressive mode. There were moments when I knew I was not to be quiet and still or to retreat. There were moments when I had to be more than assertive; I had to be overtly aggressive. Considering that the Bible says a woman is to be of gentle and quiet spirit, at what point are we given permission to act or respond aggressively? Was I supposed to drive to his home and demand that he return? Was I supposed to phone him every day and plead with him? Was I supposed to follow him everywhere he went? Was I to open his mail? Not at all!

In my case, this was a reminder from God that we war not against flesh and blood but against powers and principalities and rulers in dark places. In other words, my posture of aggression occurred during prayer: "Satan, there's no way you are going to have the victory in this situation. What God has joined together, neither you nor any man will separate."

During one of these times of spiritual warfare, while I paced in my living room praising God as worship music played loudly throughout the house, God dropped a scripture into my heart:

Simon, Simon, Satan has asked to sift you as wheat. But I have prayed for you, Simon, that your faith may not fail. And when you have turned back, strengthen your brothers. (Luke 22:31–32)

I had received a promise from God. This was also Jim's spiritual battle. Satan had asked God to sift my husband, and by doing so my husband had left our marriage. Now I knew that Jesus had been praying for him—and still was. Through my intercessions, I knew Jim's faith would prevail and that he would turn back. I didn't know when, but I knew that at some point Jim would return to his family. If I believed the entire verse, I also could rest in the promise that when Jim did return, he would be able to strengthen others around him who faced the same struggles.

So, why was I still paddling? In this instance, God was asking me to paddle. He was asking me to paddle aggressively to persevere through a series of dangerous rapids. By fighting in the spirit, our marriage was going to emerge victorious.

If I compare the story of Asa to what was happening in my marriage, I was going to be doing more than simply going out and meeting the enemy on the battlefield. I was going to have an even greater victory, because God was going to help me push back the enemy and take over some of his territory. Plus, I was going to be rewarded with plunder.

Scriptures for Reflection

Asa did what was good and right in the eyes of the Lord his God. (2 Chronicles 14:2)

_____

_____

_____

_____

_____

_____

_____

_____

Then Asa called to the Lord his God and said, "Lord, there is no we like you to help the powerless against the mighty. Help us, O Lord our God, for we rely on you, and in your name we have come against this vast army. O Lord, you are our God; do not let man prevail against you." (2 Chronicles 14:11)

_____

_____

_____

_____

_____

_____

...and Asa and his army pursued them as far as Gerar. (2 Chronicles 14:13)

_____

_____

_____

_____

PERSONAL LEADERSHIP EXAMPLE

There have been occasions at work when I've been confronted with either bullies or antagonistic co-workers. It was like they were doing everything in their power to either discourage me or make me look bad to my supervisor. After praying, it was quite clear that God didn't want me to do anything. Initially, I felt like a lamb being led to slaughter. I was going to be humiliated and cast aside. Rejected. So what did God do? God removed the bully.

Confrontation can occur in our workplaces on a regular basis, especially in the form of bullying. In one instance, an individual seemed to take great delight in storming into my department, cursing and swearing about how incompetent everyone was. My staff would quickly respond by doing whatever he asked them to do. They would drop everything, regardless of priority, to ensure this ranting individual would quiet down.

Early one morning, before most employees had arrived at the office, I went into this individual's office, closed the door behind me, and calmly sat down. No doubt, he was curious as to why I was paying him this confidential visit so early in the morning. With as much dignity and calmness as I could muster, I told him that I would no longer tolerate the way he spoke to my staff, and the way he treated them. I wouldn't tolerate bullying in the workplace. If he had an issue with anyone in my department, he needed to come directly to me so we could sit down and determine the best resolution to his issues.

I'm confident that every one of you who's reading this book has encountered a bully at some point in your life. You've probably tried all manner of trust postures, hoping he'd go away or that his behaviour would cease. However, that's not how the Bible states we are to deal with a bully. We are not to be passive and allow him or her to ride roughshod over us. We are not to retreat or back down, which would indicate their behaviour is acceptable. We are not to wait for him or her to engage us. Instead of being on the defensive, we need to respond with aggressive behaviour. In other words, we take the first step and we enter into their territory—maybe even their office.

With the power and grace of God that comes through prayer, and with Holy Spirit prompting every word we speak, a bully's weapons will be quickly disassembled. Confronting in love can be very effective. We don't need to yell, use colourful language, stomp our feet, wave our fists, or slam doors. Knowing that we war not against flesh and blood, and knowing that no weapons formed against us (in this case, bullies) will prosper, we know that we will be victorious. Greater is he who is in us than he who is in the world. Or as King Asa said, "Do not let men prevail against you, oh God."

GROUP DISCUSSION
Think of a time when you were prepared to engage the enemy in battle. After you prayed, did you experience something like King Asa, where you ended up not having to do anything at all? Did God totally intervene? Share this story with the group.

Deborah
*After Ehud died, the Israelites once again did evil in the eyes of
the Lord. So the Lord sold them into the hands of Jabin, a king of
Canaan, who reigned in Hazor. The commander of his army was
Sisera, who lived in Harosheth Haggoyim. Because he had nine
hundred iron chariots and had cruelly oppressed the Israelites for
twenty years, they cried to the Lord for help.*

*Deborah, a prophetess, the wife of Lappidoth, was leading
Israel at that time. She held court under the Palm of Deborah
between Ramah and Bethel in the hill country of Ephraim, and
the Israelites came to her to have their disputes decided. She sent
for Barak son of Abinoam from Kedesh in Naphtali and said to
him, "The Lord, the God of Israel, commands you: 'Go, take with
you ten thousand men of Naphtali and Zebulun and lead the way
to Mount Tabor. I will lure Sisera, the commander of Jabin's army,
with his chariots and his troops to the Kishon River and give him
into your hands.'"*

*Barak said to her, "If you go with me, I will go; but if you don't
go with me, I won't go."*

"Very well," Deborah said, "I will go with you. But because of the way you are going about this, the honor will not be yours, for the Lord will hand Sisera over to a woman." So Deborah went with Barak to Kedesh, where he summoned Zebulun and Naphtali. Ten thousand men followed him, and Deborah also went with him.

Now Heber the Kenite had left the other Kenites, the descendants of Hobab, Moses' brother-in-law, and pitched his tent by the great tree in Zaanannim near Kedesh.

When they told Sisera that Barak son of Abinoam had gone up to Mount Tabor, Sisera gathered together his nine hundred iron chariots and all the men with him, from Harosheth Haggoyim to the Kishon River.

Then Deborah said to Barak, "Go! This is the day the Lord has given Sisera into your hands. Has not the Lord gone ahead of you?" So Barak went down Mount Tabor, followed by ten thousand men. At Barak's advance, the Lord routed Sisera and all his chariots and army by the sword, and Sisera abandoned his chariot and fled on foot.

But Barak pursued the chariots and army as far as Harosheth Haggoyim. All the troops of Sisera fell by the sword; not a man was left. Sisera, however, fled on foot to the tent of Jael, the wife of Heber the Kenite, because there were friendly relations between Jabin king of Hazor and the clan of Heber the Kenite.

Jael went out to meet Sisera and said to him, "Come, my Lord, come right in. Don't be afraid." So he entered her tent, and she put a covering over him.

"I'm thirsty," he said. "Please give me some water." She opened a skin of milk, gave him a drink, and covered him up.

"Stand in the doorway of the tent," he told her. "If someone comes by and asks you, 'Is anyone here?' say 'No.'"

But Jael, Heber's wife, picked up a tent peg and a hammer and went quietly to him while he lay fast asleep, exhausted. She drove the peg through his temple into the ground, and he died.

Barak came by in pursuit of Sisera, and Jael went out to meet him. "Come," she said, "I will show you the man you're looking for." So he went in with her, and there lay Sisera with the tent peg through his temple—dead.

On that day God subdued Jabin, the Canaanite king, before the Israelites. And the hand of the Israelites grew stronger and stronger against Jabin, the Canaanite king, until they destroyed him.

The Song of Deborah

On that day Deborah and Barak son of Abinoam sang this song:

When the princes in Israel take the lead, when the people willingly offer themselves—praise the Lord!

"Hear this, you kings! Listen, you rulers! I will sing to the Lord, I will sing; I will make music to the Lord, the God of Israel.

"O Lord, when you went out from Seir, when you marched from the land of Edom, the earth shook, the heavens poured, the clouds poured down water. The mountains quaked before the Lord, the One of Sinai, before the Lord, the God of Israel.

"In the days of Shamgar son of Anath, in the days of Jael, the roads were abandoned; travelers took to winding paths. Village life in Israel ceased, ceased until I, Deborah, arose, arose a mother in Israel. When they chose new gods, war came to the city gates, and not a shield or spear was seen among forty thousand in Israel. My heart is with Israel's princes, with the willing volunteers among the people. Praise the Lord!" (Judges 4:1–2:9)

According to the book of Judges, Deborah was leading Israel at the time. She held court between Ramah and Bethel in the hill country of Ephraim. Israelites came to her to have their disputes settled.

This story occurs after Abraham led the Jewish people out of Egypt to their promised land. Abraham's successor, a military leader named Joshua, had died and Israel was now governed by judges, of which there were fourteen. Deborah was their fourth judge. During this era, the Israelites had forgotten all that God had done in the wilderness under Abraham's leadership. They had also forgotten all of the miraculous victories from when Joshua had conquered the foreign land and provided areas for each of the twelve tribes of Israel to live. The Israelites did evil in the sight of the Lord, so the Lord sold them into the hands of Jabin, the evil king of Canaan.

Deborah was known as a mother in Israel. Her heart was with Israel's princes and the willing volunteers among the people. At God's command, she summoned Barak, her military commander, and gave him instructions to lead their army into battle. Initially Barak didn't want to go into battle without Deborah. Finally, at Barak's insistence, Deborah agreed to accompany him. Although the story indicates that Barak may have been weak because he wouldn't go into battle without Deborah, I'd like to believe that he knew the anointing on Deborah's life and wanted to ensure that this anointing was with his army. Barak, indeed, got that assurance when Deborah said, "Go! This is the day the Lord has given Sisera into your hands. Has not the Lord gone ahead of you?"

The way in which Barak went about his request may not have been very courageous or noble. As a result, Deborah prophesied that the victory would go to a woman. At first, I was puzzled by her statement. Barak was her commander-in-chief. Why would he or one of his men not be given the victory? Surely they were well-trained men—ten thousand to be exact. Deborah's comment almost sounded spiteful, as though to say, "Fine. If you're too cowardly to lead and need a woman to go with you, then a woman will have the victory." But those weren't the thoughts going through her head. She wasn't speaking out of her own disappointment for his supposed lack of courage. She was speaking the exact words God had given her to speak. The feared leader of Jabin's army was going to be killed by a woman.

At first, we may think Deborah would have been the woman to kill Sisera. She was a warrior, after all! When reading the account, we learn that it was another woman, and not even one from Israel. Sisera was killed by the wife of Herber the Kenite, a man that King Jabin sought an alliance with. We learn from the story that the Kenites were not a logical group for Jabin to have sought an alliance with, as the Kenites were descendants of Moses' brother-in-law Horeb. That means Jabin sought an alliance with other Israelites, descendants of his sister. Herber only represented one family from this clan—a family who had rebelled against the Jewish ways and was seeking a life without the guidance of their sovereign God. Obviously, not everyone in Herber's family thought of the Canaanites in the same manner. Not everyone wanted an alliance with King Jabin. Not everyone wanted to provide a safe haven for Sisera. A woman from Herber's very household killed Sisera—his wife. We could conclude that Jael, Herber's wife, didn't have the same rebellious spirit as her husband. She aligned herself with Deborah and her Israelite ancestors.

Let us reflect for a moment on Deborah's character and her attributes. She was a judge who wisely led her community. That means she was like a prime minister or president of one of our modern-day governments. She was deemed fair and respected. Many people came to her to have their cases mediated and settled. Because of her willingness to serve her country in battle, she could be deemed patriotic. She wouldn't have been a passive patriot. She was aggressive. In other words, she demonstrated her trust in God by being a trained warrior who accompanied her commander into battle. She demonstrated her trust in God by handing over the leadership of the army to Barak. That means she trusted God enough to delegate her authority. Finally, Deborah was a prophetess. That means she knew God, knew His voice, and was obedient to that voice.

Deborah wasn't domineering, controlling, judgmental, or manipulative. She didn't operate out of her own knowledge. She operated under the strength and wisdom God gave her. She governed in a posture of aggressive trust by actively pursuing her enemy. She didn't passively sit back and wait for God to deal with her enemies. She didn't retreat from her enemy, and she didn't rely on someone else to fight her battles.

MY STORY

After Jim and I had been separated for five months, God had me read the book of Hosea. This book provides an account of one of Israel's prophets whom God called to wed a prostitute. God wanted to illustrate how the Israelites' unfaithfulness was just like that of a wayward woman.

So Why Are You Still Paddling?

No matter how many times she strayed, God would welcome her back. He would search for her and bring her back if she wouldn't come on her own accord. When I read these passages, I knew I had to destroy "the list," the list that had identified all the things God was going to have to change in Jim before I'd welcome him back into my life. Really! I was telling God what He needed to do before I would take a step of reconciliation.

I realized that I had to call Jim back into our home. Regardless of the state he was in, and regardless of where he was at in his walk with God, I had to venture out of my shell of peace and safety and ask him to come back. That meant I had to give to God all the hurts I felt. I had to forgive Jim for what he had done and ask God to give me the grace and mercy to move forward.

Thankfully, the second week of January was our traditional church-wide week of prayer and fasting. I entered into this season with a specific prayer that God would help me to love Jim just like Hosea had loved his wife, Gomer. Regardless of what his wife had done, Hosea had been asked by God to bring her back. This meant that regardless of what Jim had done, I had to bring him back. I wasn't to wait passively at home any longer for a reconciliation of our relationship.

I was not to simply prepare myself for the day of his return. This was more than me being spiritually filled and physically fit and attractive in all the natural ways. This was about more than getting myself back into shape, about more than dressing nicely every day and ensuring my make-up was properly applied, about more than being friendly and hospitable. This was an aggressive posture of trust where I had to step out in faith and ask Jim to come home.

At the end of the week, Jim took our son to an out-of-town hockey tournament. That meant I had a couple of additional days to seek the Lord for His wisdom, and His good and perfect timing for when I was to ask Jim to return to our family home. When Sunday evening came and Jim dropped Brandon off, I quoted the same sentence that one of my previous examples, Esther, had said to her king. Like Esther, I stepped out in faith and asked if I could prepare a meal for my estranged husband. That was all. No talk of reconciliation—only an invitation for supper.

Like Deborah, I aggressively went out and faced the enemy. Only instead of using a battle sword, I used the sword of kindness. I asked my husband to have a meal with his family the following Friday evening.

Needless to say, the following five days were very interesting. My emotions went from one extreme to another. What had I done? Why on earth would I want my husband at our dinner table for a family meal? How could I possibly forgive him for abandoning me? Well, God rewarded my obedience. My posture of aggressive trust was rewarded by the hand of God miraculously intervening and saving our marriage.

When Jim arrived at our door that Friday evening, the first words out of his mouth were, "I want to come home. Will you have me?"

I asked him one simple question: "Why?" He responded that he was a better man with me than without me. In other words, God was going to continue to do His good and perfect work in my husband while we were under the same roof. Although there wasn't an indication that anything in Jim had changed, I knew our family being back together again was the right thing. I knew that as I allowed God to continue to work in and through me, Jim would eventually become the man of God he was called to be. I wasn't going to receive him back as a perfect vessel ready to serve God in global missions or full-time ministry.

I wasn't gaining a transformed husband who would embrace his role as priest of our family. I had to see with God's eyes, in faith and with full and complete trust that God's ways aren't my ways and that His purposes are higher than my purposes. Little did I know how exciting the journey ahead of us was going to be.

Take a moment and reflect upon your own marriage. No matter what your spouse has or hasn't done, are you able to forgive him or her? Are you able to act with God's love, grace, and mercy to extend your arm of kindness with dignity? Can you be aggressive in your posture of trusting God and go into the enemy's camp to take back what Satan has stolen from you? Regardless of the condition of what God gives back to you, are you able to love unconditionally—just like Hosea loved Gomer?

Scriptures for Reflection

She sent for Barak son of Abinoam from Kedesh in Naphtali and said to him, "The Lord, the God of Israel, commands you: 'Go, take with you ten thousand men of Naphtali and Zebulun and lead the way to Mount Tabor. I will lure Sisera, the commander of Jabin's army, with his chariots and his troops to the Kishon River and give him into your hands.'" (Judges 4:6–7)

_____

_____

_____

_____

_____

_____

...in the days of Jael, the roads were abandoned; travelers took to winding paths. Village life in Israel ceased, ceased until I, Deborah, arose, arose a mother in Israel. (Judges 5:6–7)

_____

_____

_____

_____

_____

So may all your enemies perish, O Lord! But may they who love you be like the sun when it rises in its strength. (Judges 5:31)

_____

_____

_____

_____

_____

PERSONAL LEADERSHIP EXAMPLE

During my thirty-year career, I've held various positions of leadership where trusting God has become a matter of course. I pray for His wisdom, knowledge, and understanding before I walk into my workplace every day. I pray before I go into any leadership meeting or discussion with directors of the board. Although I've been labelled a type-A personality, I generally find it very easy to trust God in all manners of postures. I have learned to be patient and wait for God to intervene. I have accepted the fact that there are some things I cannot change, times when I need to step back and retreat from the situation. These are the times when I must not paddle.

I have learned to be active in the exercising of my faith by trusting God as I prepare for the steps ahead. At times, I learn to be more skilled in my paddling technique. Trusting God in an assertive or confrontational posture has probably been one of my most difficult postures. Paddling your canoe to please God isn't the same as paddling your canoe to please man. Like most people, I want to be liked and respected. Stepping out of my comfort zone and acting aggressively isn't a posture I often display in the workplace.

There have been a few times when I knew being aggressive was the right way to portray my trust in God and not fear man. Like Deborah leading her army into battle, I knew I had to step out and take back what the enemy had taken from me. In many of my governance roles, I needed to be able to confront those at the table who had unfounded beliefs about what was happening in the organization. I needed to take a stand for what was right, true, and pure. Whether it was at a board meeting or committee meeting, there have been times when I knew that what I was compelled to say would go against the thoughts of the majority in the room.

Trusting God with an aggressive posture means making those difficult and unpopular decisions that bring about better results for the organization. For example, in one organization, it meant that I had to put a halt to a year-end inventory count because it wasn't being conducted with the proper controls in place. It meant that I sometimes had to actively engage in the release of very capable staff during a company's restructuring. Aggressively trusting God will ultimately gain you respect, because it means you're prepared to make the tough decisions. It shows that you don't fear the thoughts and opinions of man, but rather the calling and purposes of God.

Sometimes my posture of trusting God for a raise in salary didn't mean sitting back and waiting. I had to actually approach my boss and ask for the raise. I didn't ask in a demanding or spiteful manner. With facts in hand and the promptings of Holy Spirit, I pled my case for what was fair and just.

In positions of leadership, remember that we are not to be domineering, manipulative, judgmental, and full of our own "textbook" knowledge.

If God has given us a career, we must remember to operate with His wisdom. We must obtain our wisdom from His word. We must be inspirational to those around us and be an encouragement within our sphere of influence. God wants us to rebuke indifference and apathy. He wants us to rise up and speak for justice. We are to be meditative and conciliatory in our approach to workplace conflicts.

GROUP DISCUSSION

Share with the group a situation in your workplace when you knew you had to make an unpopular decision. What was the outcome? Why did God ask you to paddle?

WHY DO YOU TRUST? | 14

We've spent the last ten chapters studying different postures of trust which have been demonstrated by ten different men and women. In some situations, God tells us to trust Him through retreat. We may have picked up our paddles and paddled backwards, or we may have laid down the paddles and allowed God to take us in reverse. In some cases, we trust God by laying down our paddles and passively waiting for God to intervene. In other situations, we learn how to be more skilled in using our paddles so we are better able to manoeuvre out of our circumstances. Then there are those situations when God gives us permission to paddle, and in some cases paddle quite aggressively.

In each of these illustrations, God gives us promises for trusting Him. Conversely, God has also stated that there are consequences for not trusting Him. We may not get it right the first time we get into the canoe and pick up the paddles. We may choose to paddle when God tells us to be still. We may elect to do nothing when God prompts us to paddle a bit harder. When God tells us to persevere, we may back away and retreat… or we may even get out of the canoe. Even by making the wrong choices, we still learn how to trust God.

Each of us will experience the consequences for our wrong choices. As I indicated in an earlier chapter, God disciplines those whom He loves and calls His sons. Through this discipline, we learn obedience. Just as we, as parents, discipline our earthly children when they make wrong choices or are disobedient, God disciplines us. We may not welcome the firm hand of God, but we'll be thankful for it in the end. If we aren't disciplined for our mistakes, how will we ever learn? Without knowing the boundaries in which God allows us to operate, we would never know or appreciate His wonderful promises.

I've taken the liberty of providing additional scripture references on trusting God. I have provided references to what will happen when we choose to trust God (to not paddle) and what will happen when we choose to be in control (to paddle). Take a moment and mediate on these verses. Do any of them remind you of a situation you were in?

Take a moment and consider the ten biblical leaders we have studied. Imagine what the outcome would have been had they not trusted God. What would the consequences have been to themselves, their families, their relationships, their workplaces, and the organizations (countries) they led?

Reflect upon these same individuals and consider the rewards God gave them. What promises were fulfilled? In the following table, take a moment to add your own comments in each of the sections.

	Consequence	Promise
Esther	Jewish people would have been killed.	She would become queen.
Daniel		
Elisha		
Mary		
David		
Ruth		
Hezekiah		
Abigail		
Asa		
Deborah		

Scriptures for Reflection: Consequences

But the Lord said to Moses and Aaron, "Because you did not trust in me enough to honor me as holy in the sight of the Israelites, you will not bring this community into the land I give them." (Numbers 20:12)

_____

_____

_____

_____

_____

_____

This is what the Lord says: "Cursed is the one who trusts in man, who depends on flesh for his strength and whose heart turns away from the Lord." (Jeremiah 17:5)

_____

_____

_____

_____

_____

_____

Since you trust in your deeds and riches, you too will be taken captive, and Chemosh will go into exile, together with his priests and officials. (Jeremiah 48:7)

_____

_____

_____

_____

_____

_____

WHY DO YOU TRUST?

If I tell the righteous man that he will surely live, but then he trusts in his righteousness and does evil, none of the righteous things he has done will be remembered; he will die for the evil he has done. (Ezekiel 33:13)

_____

_____

_____

_____

_____

So if you have not been trustworthy in handling worldly wealth, who will trust you with true riches? (Luke 16:11)

_____

_____

_____

_____

And if you have not been trustworthy with someone else's property, who will give you property of your own? (Luke 16:12)

_____

_____

_____

_____

_____

Scriptures for Reflection: Promises

Many are the woes of the wicked, but the Lord's unfailing love surrounds the man who trusts in him. (Psalm 32:10)

Trust in the Lord and do good; dwell in the land and enjoy safe pasture. (Psalm 37:3)

Blessed is the man who makes the Lord his trust, who does not look to the proud, to those who turn aside to false gods. (Psalm 40:4)

But I am like an olive tree flourishing in the house of God; I trust in God's unfailing love for ever and ever. (Psalm 52:8)

146

O Lord Almighty, blessed is the man who trusts in you. (Psalm 84:12)

_____

_____

_____

_____

He will have no fear of bad news; his heart is steadfast, trusting in the Lord. (Psalm 112:7)

_____

_____

_____

Those who trust in the Lord are like Mount Zion, which cannot be shaken but endures forever. (Psalm 125:1)

_____

_____

_____

Whoever gives heed to instruction prospers, and blessed is he who trusts in the Lord. (Proverbs 16:20)

_____

_____

_____

_____

A greedy man stirs up dissension, but he who trusts in the Lord will prosper. (Proverbs 28:25)

_____

_____

_____

_____

_____

Fear of man will prove to be a snare, but whoever trusts in the Lord is kept safe. (Proverbs 29:25)

_____

_____

_____

_____

_____

You will keep in perfect peace him whose mind is steadfast, because he trusts in you. (Isaiah 26:3)

_____

_____

_____

_____

_____

But blessed is the man who trusts in the Lord, whose confidence is in him. (Jeremiah 17:7)

_____

_____

_____

_____

_____

The Lord is good, a refuge in times of trouble. He cares for those who trust in him… (Nahum 1:7)

_____

_____

_____

_____

Whoever can be trusted with very little can also be trusted with much, and whoever is dishonest with very little will also be dishonest with much. (Luke 16:10)

_____

_____

_____

_____

As the Scripture says, "Anyone who trusts in him will never be put to shame." (Romans 10:11)

_____

_____

_____

_____

May the God of hope fill you with all joy and peace as you trust in him, so that you may overflow with hope by the power of the Holy Spirit. (Romans 15:13)

_____

_____

_____

_____

GROUP DISCUSSION

Share with the group an example of when you didn't trust God. What was the consequence? Share with the group a promise that God fulfilled in your life because you chose to trust Him and not take control.

CONCLUSION

Can you identify with any of these men and women? Do you wish to be a woman of inspiration like Deborah, but you're afraid people will perceive you as being domineering and judgmental? Has God put you in a place where meditative skills are required? How do you paddle in this situation?

Are you in a situation where you need to lead as King Asa led—courageously, confidently, and with conviction?

Do you desire to be like Ruth—a handmaiden? Are you in a pace of servitude where you must honour and walk in obedience? Do you wish to be known for your constant and dependable character and industrious nature? Does this posture of trust require a consistent, uninterrupted routine of paddling?

Has God ever asked you to retreat or step away from a situation, relationship, or position you may have been offered? There may be times when you're offered a position of advancement in your company but you know you cannot honour God by accepting it, as doing so will compromise your beliefs. Laying down your paddles and getting out of the canoe is a difficult posture of trust, especially if you're unfamiliar with the shore on which you find yourself.

Are you in a spiritual spa, like Esther, where God is taking time to clean you up, on the inside and out? Have you learned to pray and intercede for those less fortunate? Have you been given a position of favour? If so, is your light shining and are you being used for God's glory? Perhaps there are no paddles in your canoe and none within your reach.

Have you been falsely accused? Are you facing "twelve angry men"? Are you able to lay down the paddles of what is seemingly right, just, and true and not defend yourself? Can you trust God enough to defend you even when you're locked in the pit with hungry lions?

Are you like Abigail? Maybe you're married to an unbeliever! You must continue to honour your husband (or wife), but you must honour God as well. You don't know what may become of your unbelieving spouse. In the meantime, are you providing for the poor and the orphan? Do you possess good judgment in your workplace? Are you walking with dignity? Are you becoming more skilled in the use of your paddles?

Has God ever placed you in a situation where you needed to rely on the counsel of those around you? Like King Hezekiah, did wisdom, knowledge, understanding, strategy, and tactics come from the prophetic people in your life? Did their advice make sense? Was it profitable?

Finally, are you trying to be like Mary—learning to rest at the feet of Jesus? Perhaps you don't wish to be anxious about tomorrow, but instead wish to be known as a worshipper, someone who is disciplined in the works of God. By being passive, you're not picking up the paddles, even though they're in the canoe at your feet.

Has God ever asked you to sit in the canoe and do nothing? Just like Elisha, as he sat on the hill as the enemy advanced against him, you're not the least bit anxious about what may happen. You are at perfect peace because your mind, heart, and soul are steadfast on the Lord.

Let God take you, as His ambassadors, and renew a right spirit in you. May He place you in positions where you may be an influencer. May He place you in positions of servitude where you may be industrious and hard-working for His kingdom. May He place you in high places where your light will shine. May God place you into esteemed positions for such a time as this. May God use you to be a conciliator, capable and dignified in whatever role you have been placed. Finally, let God make you into a worshipper, where you can choose to sit at His feet and not be caught up in the busyness of life. May God use you in every relationship and in every workplace setting in the posture of trust He has called you to embody in that season.

Although I have come through seasons of trust, I've also realized that learning trust isn't a one-time lesson. New and very different seasons of trusting God happen constantly throughout our lives. During each of these times, the depth of that trust changes, and our posture changes along with it.

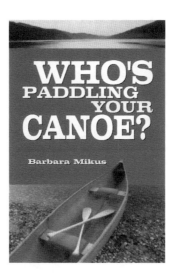

The journey through our Christian life can be compared to a canoe expedition down a river. During this voyage, we are each passengers with Jesus guiding the vessel. The canoe leaving the shore illustrates salvation. Learning to paddle in the rapids illustrates perseverance. Various stops along the shore illustrate discipleship, forgiveness and trust.

The successful surrender of the paddles at various times indicates who is in control as we learn about other Christian attributes such as patience, honour, love, joy and hope. Add to this the need for relationships and the desire to be involved in Ministry and the reader will have an exciting journey. Different events along the voyage represent specific stages in our lives when we need to make choices. The results are based upon who is paddling the canoe. The journey can take as long as required or not be completed at all.

Whether you read this book as part of your personal devotions or work through it as part of a Group Bible Study, the reader will be impacted by how the power of God influenced who was ultimately in control of our author's life.